# Earthquakes, Tsunamis & Floods, Oh My!

## An Emergency Preparedness Guidebook

### Loa Kirk Andersen

Note to readers: This book has been written and published strictly for informational purposes and in no way should be used as a substitute for actual instruction with qualified professionals. The author and publisher are providing you with information in this work so that you can have the knowledge and can choose, at your own risk, to act on that knowledge.

Any use of this information in this book is made on the reader's good judgment. The author and publisher assume no liability for perusal injury, property damage, consequential damage or loss, however caused, from using the information in this book.

## Publisher's Comment
### *How This Title Came About*

Now, please let us explain a bit about how the title of this book came about.

Loa often writes articles for others to use under their own names. It's called 'ghost writing.' She had carefully crafted a rather lighthearted, 400-word article for a client who sold walkie talkies about a child temporarily lost in the Uinta Mountains of Utah and how the mother feared for the child's safety. She used this sentence: Thoughts of the dangers assailed my mind; steep cliffs, a raging stream, lions and tigers and bears, oh, my!

The client responded, "They don't have lions and tigers in the Uinta Mountains. Maybe use cougars and wolves and drop the 'oh, my'. Obviously, he wasn't a fan of "The Wizard of Oz." It struck us hilariously funny at the time, but we thought we'd better warn our readers.

Loa uses many literary references, mostly from films, plays, and commercials, to illustrate a point...or just to be clever. At least, she thinks she's being clever. If perchance you miss the meaning, you're probably much younger than Loa, or more seriously inclined. If that happens, just skip it and keep reading. We won't mind.

You may, in this book, find any or all of the following:

- o "As you wish..." *Princess Bride*
- o "Thank you for doing this, Ellen." *Dave*
- o "Can you hear me now?" Commercial for phone service ...I forget which one!
- o "Frankly, Scarlett...." *Gone with the Wind*
- o "There's trouble, right here in River City." *Music Man*

Loa used that latter reference once in a talk. Afterwards, a sweet little lady tugged on her sleeve and whispered, "I know you travel a lot, but you're not in River City right now. This is Seattle."

Ah, so…

Now…on to the serious stuff.

# About the Author

I have been a 'wanderer' most of my life. As a result, I learned when very young the importance of carrying basic necessities in my carry-all. I never knew when I would be stuck in an airport, in some out-of-the-way place, or in a primitive area where necessities were scarce. I also learned how to improvise or do without.

I became passionate about emergency preparation as a result of seeing the problems created by the Marysville-Yuba City floods in 1955. Since then, I've experienced three earthquakes, two major floods, and one volcanic eruption first-hand. I've served as a first responder, speaker/educator, and as a member of CERT. Currently, I'm a CERT instructor in the Tacoma-Gig Harbor area.

My education as an emergency preparation specialist has come from hands-on experience as well as classroom training through FEMA/Citizens Corp.

An ardent advocate of emergency preparedness, I am eager to share my knowledge with anyone who will listen…or to convert those who don't wish to listen!

I'm a freelance writer, public speaker, and substitute teacher. In my spare time, I'm a veracious reader, love to sea-kayak among whales and am an avid genealogist.

# Contents

## Part 1: Philosophy

## Part 2: Bare Bones Basics

## Part 3: In 500 words or less

# PART ONE:  INTRODUCTION

Oh, I've heard about this preparedness stuff for years and nothing
has happened…well, not here, anyway."

"I can last for three days.  Then someone will come to help me!"

"Yikes, I know I should, but it's so confusing.  I don't know
where to start!"

"Oh, brother.  Another book about emergency preparation.  How
boring!"

We've all heard these statements. Perhaps we've even said one or two
or something similar, especially the last one about e-prep being boring.
I've said that one myself…but, in my defense, I was very young and
very naive when I said it!

Let's face it. Some people don't prepare for emergencies or hard times
because the prospect of dealing with them is too frightening. Others
are overwhelmed by the sheer magnitude of the endeavor. Others are
convinced that preparation for an unknown event isn't really necessary
and subscribe to the 'grasshopper' lifestyle. A few (including me) find
the talk of doom and gloom quite unsettling, while others find the
entire subject of emergency preparations totally boring.

So why have I written a book about it? After all, there are a gazillion
books out there on prepping and many more sites on the internet that
discuss it. Unfortunately, most fall into one of two categories. Some are
so doom and gloomy, they are simply too scary and overwhelming to
read. The others are factual, contain good information, but are so dry
it's hard to read them without (yawn) falling asleep. I decided that an

easy-to-read book with a lighthearted approach to preparedness might be appropriate.

I'm convinced that a huge percentage of the general population is terribly uninformed about emergency preparation. For example, shortly after the 2010 earthquake in Haiti, I was standing in line at the bank when I happened to overhear the following conversation.

"If an earthquake like that happens here, I'll just call 911," commented one well-dressed lady." (My silent comment: Like 50,000 others won't be trying to do the same thing?)

Her friend replied, "Things like that don't happen here. They only happen in poor countries." (My wide-eyed but-silent comment: You've got to be kidding!)

The last of the trio then added, "I'd like do something, but I don't have a clue where to begin." (My epiphany: Aha, now there's an idea!)

I immediately contacted the editor of a weekly newspaper, the Gig Harbor Life. I arranged to write a column on emergency preparation geared to those who may be slightly interested in the subject, but who were not sufficiently motivated to research the information on the internet. That day, my column, "Just in Case" was born.

Surprisingly, it has been quite successful; it's even gone viral. If comments are any indication, people have discovered through the column that emergency preparedness can be interesting, cost-effective, practical, and even fun! Yes, my writing is a bit "cotton candy"…fluffy, lighthearted, and sometimes a bit silly, but it still contains basic information, sensible tips, and practical ideas for becoming prepared.

Preparedness is much more than just food storage. It is self-sufficiency. It is being in control in out-of-control situations. Being prepared doesn't make the crisis disappear; it just makes it more manageable. Practical preparedness now could very well make the difference between coping and chaos.

Personally, I have a hard time handling chaos. I'm stressed if my double light switches have one switch down and the other up! Chaos is not my "thing" so I'm preparing my home and car so that they are safe havens in times of crisis…any crisis! This could be anything from getting stuck on the freeway during a snowstorm, loss of employment, a major earthquake, or a complete economic meltdown. It could be even aliens landing in my front yard, but I admit the chances of that are pretty remote so I don't suggest spending much time worrying about that!

Of course, one can't prepare for everything, but being a little bit prepared is a whole lot better than not being prepared at all. Being well prepared is even better!

I'm not suggesting that you turn your home into a fortress nor that you become so obsessed with what "might" happen that you forget to enjoy living now.

Instead, I hope you will learn the principles of preparedness and determine what will work for you and your family. Then just do it! Do what is necessary, one step at a time, with a personalized plan of action.

It is time to quit closing your eyes, crossing your fingers and hoping that all will be well. Now is the time to prepare. There is a small window of time when preparation is possible. After that window closes, the time for preparation will be over.

Incidentally, I do suggest that you don't advertise your preparations. For my reasoning on this, please read the article #14 under the section "500 Words or Less" at the end of this manual.

## Emergency?  Disaster? What's the Difference?

First, let's talk definitions. What is the difference between an emergency and a disaster?  Admittedly, in layman's experience, there isn't much difference. For my purposes, an <u>emergency</u> is any unplanned event that can cause death, losses, or significant injuries to those involved. An emergency can shut down businesses, disrupt operations, and cause suffering. However, I generally think of emergencies as time-limited. They are situations that most local first responders or individuals can handle and the dangers associated with the emergency are dispersed within a fairly short period of time.

A <u>disaster,</u> on the other hand, causes profound damage to our society. The damage or losses may be that of human life, property, or affect the environment. In a true disaster, the population affected is taken by profound shock. FEMA defines a disaster as "A serious disruption of the functioning of society, causing widespread human, material, or environmental losses which exceed the ability of affected society to copy using only its own resources."

In a disaster, the local first responders are overwhelmed and unable to assist all those who may need attention. Please read that statement once more, as it is critical to those new to preparedness.

If a disaster happens in your area, most likely the police, firemen, hospital staff, and utility workers will be overwhelmed. That means no one will answer a 911 call, no fire trucks will come roaring down your driveway eager to assist, and medical attention may be non-existent for days, weeks, or longer.

This situation is called the YOYO condition. YOYO: You're On Your Own. This is why I promote preparedness…so you will be able to care for yourself, your family, and when possible, assist your neighbors as well.

This manual is the first in a series and will get you started on the road to total preparedness. It will walk you through the initial steps required to become reasonably self-sufficient for short term emergencies. It is geared for those who are just becoming interested in preparedness as well as for those who have questions about basic prepping.

The second manual will assist the reader to cope with a disaster of a longer duration. It will detail how to develop skills such as purifying water, planning extended food storage, and much more. The third discusses long-term preparedness, since some disasters may last a year or more, creating a 'new normal.'

Hopefully, this series will entertain, entice, inform and instruct you in the fine art of becoming prepared for emergencies.  Okay, maybe 'fine art' is a bit much, but you get the idea!

## The Why and Wherefore of Disaster Planning

**Be prepared.** These two simple words have a wide range of meaning. To one, it could be having a candle and a few matches in the kitchen junk drawer. To another, it could entail purchasing acreage out in the middle of nowhere and setting up an off-the-grid compound complete with barbed wire fences and lots of fire power.

Somewhere between these two extremes is your comfort zone. You…and you alone…must decide just how much emergency preparations you wish to take. No one else can make that decision for you.

Disaster shows have become extremely popular recently. We've gleefully watched massive destruction due to global warming, a new ice age covering North America in just a few days, aliens determined to wipe all humans off the planet, and meteors on a collision course with Earth. In each scenario, the human race is 'saved' by the likes of Bruce Willis or John Cusack. These shows are exciting, entertaining, and very predictable. It's always the lone rejected, misunderstood scientist-rebel who single-handedly saves the day. We are guaranteed that all will end well in approximately one hour and forty-five minutes…or at least before our pizza gets cold.

Unfortunately, a real crisis is not like the fictionalized scenes we see on the screen. Think back to the actual, real-life footage of 9/11, the aftermath of the earthquake in Haiti, or the tsunami that inundated Miyako in Tohoku's Iwate Prefecture and which, in the Sendai area, traveled up to six miles inland. Those scenes were terrifying as well as heartbreaking. The carnage never seemed to stop. Lives were changed forever; many…far too many…were lost.

Survival in a real crisis is emotionally and physically demanding. In real life, no handsome film star will ride to the rescue on his white horse, his Harley, or on a jet ski. Recent experience has shown that 'the government' will not be available to hold your hand either…at least not immediately.

FEMA has stated, "If a disaster threatens your community, local government and disaster-relief organizations will try to help you. But you need to be prepared as well. Local officials may be overwhelmed after a major disaster and emergency personnel may not be able to reach you right away."

This means that <u>you</u> will be responsible for the immediate safety and welfare of your family. You must arm yourself with knowledge from reliable sources and adapt all that information to your specific family needs and conditions.

The time to prepare is now. It is vital to obtain necessary knowledge, skills, and supplies before a crisis occurs. This can make the difference between chaos and control, confusion and confidence. The wrong time to try to learn skills or to gather supplies is <u>during</u> an emergency. When the crisis is at your door, it's simply too late for preparation.

This manual will help you develop and implement a family preparedness plan, whether you have a huge extended family nearby or if you are single individual living alone. It will also entice, encourage, guide and push you to learn the skills that will assist you to survive whatever life may toss your direction.

Now, don't let anyone frighten you into thinking that everything must be done all at once or that you should spend huge amounts of money or go into debt to achieve your objectives. That isn't advisable nor is it necessary. You will find that by following the suggestions outlined herein, you will start with small goals that over time, will add up to a well-developed preparedness program.

Remember, you must not rely on outside agencies to rescue you in the event of a disaster. <u>You</u> are your family's first responder. They are <u>your</u> responsibility. Being prepared will bring a sense of security, confidence and offer independence from having to rely on others for your needs.

## Why I'm a "Prepper"

I don't know your reasons for reading this manual, or why you are interested in emergency preparation. However, I can tell you why I am a preparedness aficionado.

I don't like to be cold, wet, or uncomfortable. I don't like to be hungry or thirsty. I also don't like to sleep sitting up, eat cold food that normally should be hot, or… horror of horrors… go even one day without face cream, hand lotion, and toothpaste

I don't like to be without things I consider necessities: hot food, shampoo, a comfortable bed, and lemon drops. Most of all, I don't want to ever be in a position where I have to stand in a long line for basic necessities being handed out by the government nor do I want to be required to live in an emergency shelter with a whole bunch of strangers.

The foregoing are reasons that started me on the path to becoming a prepper…one who is seriously preparing for emergency situations…but one experience really brought the entire subject into sharp focus. The situation in which I found myself literally changed the direction of my life. Here's what happened.

Shortly after I moved to Gig Harbor, a major ice storm hit Washington State with a vengeance. The power went out almost immediately and stayed out for eight long, dark, wretchedly cold days. Those horrible days seemed like an eternity.

At that time, I must confess, I was woefully unprepared. My pellet stove, of course, didn't work without power. The few flashlights I managed to find among the unpacked boxes died after two days, and oh, how I longed to have a hot meal. A neighbor invited me to her house, since she had both a wood heating stove and propane cook stove. Gratefully, I packed my sleeping bag, gathered a few necessities, and trotted over to her warm, welcoming home.

It didn't take long for me to realize that our personalities were vastly different.

I had become accustomed to living alone, mostly in total silence. Although I enjoy music, I prefer my own thoughts over background noise, so only play music if I wish to seriously sit and listen to it. I'm a "silence is golden" type person. I'm also a clean freak. If there is one dirty dish in my sink, I consider my entire kitchen to be a mess, I never leave home without making my bed, and 'clutter' is an obscene word.

My neighbor had five children, five indoor pets (two dogs and three cats) and was much more relaxed regarding housekeeping. Additionally, she'd kindly invited several other families to share her cozy home. I was warm and well-fed, but I was overwhelmed by the chaos and clutter.

After one night, I returned to my cold, dark and dreary house. I realized that for me, living in close quarters with numerous strangers, no matter how congenial they are, is not an option.

That experience taught me something else that is vitally important. I learned that I am mentally and emotionally unequipped to <u>ever</u> live, however briefly, in a government-run shelter along with 500 or more other folks sleeping in the same area, doing without any semblance of privacy, and sharing limited toilet facilities! Eeeau!

## Wouldn't you like to be a Prepper too? (That's A "Prepper", not a Pepper)

How about you? Do you consider the idea of living in a government-run shelter a grand adventure? Can you imagine yourself doing without basic necessities, perhaps for weeks? Do you think eating only oatmeal three times a day is a clever new diet or does the very idea sound distasteful?

Think back to the aftermath of Katrina, specifically the scenes of public shelters that repeatedly bombarded our senses. Remember the haphazard rows of cots with personal items strewed willy-nilly on the floor? Remember the piles of trash, the disgusting bathrooms, the anger and frustration written on the faces of those 'survivors' who glared at incredibly invasive TV cameras? Remember the desperation of those who had no other place to go?

If the idea of surviving in a government-run shelter doesn't appeal to you, or if you don't like the idea of going without basic necessities, then perhaps you should be a prepper too!

## More than 72 Hours!

General disaster readiness calls for a three-day supply of food and water. Personally, I think that is Ho'omalimali. That's an Island word for fancy talk or flattery…sometimes known as "bull-_ _ _ _ ". Most emergency preparedness experts state that 72 hours is woefully insufficient. Rather, they recommend storing supplies for three weeks at a <u>minimum</u>.

"But," you say, "I thought we only had to plan for a mere 72 hours! By then, surely someone would come to help us."

Sorry, Charlie, it just doesn't happen that way.

I once attended a FEMA planning conference held in Tacoma, Washington. A FEMA executive stated quite firmly that in the event of a major disaster, FEMA would take at least <u>several days</u> just to get ready to come to the stricken area. FEMA first has to be invited by local government, which delays the process, and then they must get their folks together and organized. Once they actually arrive in the disaster zone, it takes additional time for them to settle in, set up tracking programs and accommodations for their volunteers, deliver supplies, and so forth.

Then the FEMA representative looked right at me and said, "And we won't be coming to Gig Harbor. We'll go where we can do the most good for the most people…Seattle, Tacoma, and Olympia."

Did you get that? If you don't live in a highly populated area, FEMA isn't coming your way at all.

Remember Hurricane Sandy? Six days after the storm hit, I listened to a newscaster on CNN say that people on Staten Island were angry because FEMA was assisting recovery efforts in Manhattan, but no help had yet arrived on Staten Island. This was six days after Sandy hit. SIX DAYS.

This is fact each of us must face. In the event of a <u>major disaster,</u> nobody is going to rescue us in that magic 72 hours we keep hearing about…and probably not in several weeks. No government responders, no military rescuers, no cowboys in white hats. It's truly is a YOYO situation: You're On Your Own.

Furthermore, you may be required to be a 'first responder' to your family, loved ones, or neighbors. There will be chaos. Normal emergency facilities will be overwhelmed. It's vitally important that you realize you <u>will</u> be on your own. You <u>must not</u> think that someone else will help you, and you must plan accordingly.

In a major disaster, commercial enterprises will shut down, as will many community services. There will be no running to MacDonald's or Taco Bell, no getting gas at the service stations, no 911 responders at your beck and call. It's possible that when you turn on the faucet, no water will magically appear and toilets may not flush. Most importantly, grocery stores will either be closed, refuse to take anything but cash, or the shelves will simply be empty, due to desperate people grabbing anything and everything they could until nothing is left.

## Why Doesn't the General Public Plan?

Individual and family preparedness planning is crucial to disaster readiness. Remember, in a large scale disaster, average citizens may become first responders for an extended period of time as the emergency systems become overwhelmed or incapacitated.

It is difficult to persuade people to prepare for the possibility of sheltering in place for three days. Suggesting a three-week to three-month stockpile creates even a greater challenge. Sadly, the general public remains stubbornly unprepared for even the smallest of emergencies.

There seems to be a wide-spread refusal to even consider the idea that things are changing rapidly in our world, some of which could be detrimental to our health, life, or the pursuit of a new iPod.

We watch films that portray the end of the world as we know it such as "2012." We shiver deliciously as we watch fictionalized stories of killer tornadoes, super calderas in Montana, asteroids, earthquakes, volcanic eruptions, and solar storms. Yet, we ignore the idea that some of these films are based on real possiblities. Do we want to think of that?

Nope! Of course not. We have other 'real' problems to occupy our minds: mortgages, credit card bills, clothes for kids who insist on growing, ever-rising food and gasoline prices, escapades of celebrities and politicians. We simply choose not to think of a disaster that might change our lives.

## The Power of Choice

An old English proverb states, "You pays your penny and you takes your choice." Basically, this means that people should make their own choices. With disasters, we can't choose what may happen or when it may happen, but we <u>can</u> choose how we prepare for those emergencies.

Eventually, the area in which you live will experience some kind of disaster. It may be an earthquake since <u>not one state</u> in our precious country is immune from earthquakes. It may be a massive eruption with devastating lahars if you live near one of the many volcanos that dot the western portion of our nation. Maybe it will be a prolonged ice storm, major flooding, another massive hurricane, a pandemic, or a national crisis with economic woes, infrastructure collapse or food shortages. It could also be a very personal emergency such as an unexpected illness, job loss or a nasty divorce.

Today, you have a choice. You can choose to prepare, or you can say, "That won't happen here...not to me," and do nothing. It really is just that simple.

If you are prepared when an emergency situation arises, you are better able to weather the storm, care for your loved ones, and serve others in need. If you aren't prepared, you will have chosen chaos over order, fear over confidence, and panic over prudence.

Which would you rather be: prepared and have nothing happen or be unprepared and regret it?

I'm assuming since you are reading this book, you have chosen to be prepared. That's a good thing.

## Levels of Preparedness

Preparedness is really in the eye of the beholder. Some people consider themselves prepared for anything because they have several flashlights scattered around their house, a case of bottled water, and some wood for their fireplace. Others are those similar to the folks featured on the TV series, Doomsday Preppers. These are serious preppers whose preparedness lies on the opposite end of the spectrum from those I first mentioned.

I recently watched an episode of Doomsday Preppers and came away rather depressed. The producers seem to present their subjects as doom and gloom crazies who are anticipating the 'end of the world as we know it.' Yes, some are more extreme than most and many of us cannot relate to their activities...or can't afford to emulate them.

However, there are also thousands of normal people across the United States who are quietly preparing for disasters that might occur. They prepare for possible earthquakes, wildfires, hurricanes, floods, and droughts. They learn new skills, become CERT volunteers, and make emergency contingency plans. Are they extremists? No. Are they prudent? Yes. Are they preppers? Absolutely.

There is always the specter of major events that could dramatically affect our entire nation: economic collapse, bank failures, food shortages, riots and wars as anticipated by doomsday preppers. There are concerns regarding increasingly violent weather, severe droughts, and solar flares.

Remember, however, the fewer people who are affected by an event, the more likely it is to occur to an individual. In other words, there's more chance you'll lose your job, experience a divorce, or endure local flooding than experience the eruption of a super volcano. So don't become so concerned about that super volcano that you forget to plan for a bad winter storm.

Should we prepare for the unexpected? Absolutely. We purchase car, home, and life insurance as a matter of course. Why should learning survival skills and gathering emergency supplies for possible disasters any different? Preparedness is simply another type of insurance.

My goal in writing this manual is to provide information regarding the basics for those just starting to prepare, offer suggestions for those who have passed the beginning stages, and perhaps even present new material to those who consider themselves extremely prepared for anything.

Incidentally, I've met some people who are so concerned...and scared...about what might happen tomorrow that they forget to take pleasure in today. Don't let thoughts of disaster consume every waking moment. Yes, there's trouble right here in River City, but nevertheless, opt for a more balanced approach. Plan for tomorrow but take pleasure in today.

I am not a "doom and gloom" type person. I don't accept every conspiracy theory as fact; I don't think the world will end on a specific date. Rather, I'm more like Nellie Forbush in the play, "South Pacific." I am a cockeyed optimist.

Remember the Rule of Three that prioritizes emergency needs in a survival situation. An adult may survive three minutes without air, three hours without shelter, three days without water, and three weeks without food. I'd like to add one more item: hope. I think one can survive only three seconds without hope…hope in the future and in the basic goodness and resiliency of mankind.

Plan, purchase and prepare, but don't forget to hope for the best. Without hope, everything else is irrelevant.

## Okay, Let's Prepare…But for What?

Floods, hurricanes, earthquakes, tornados, pandemics, volcanic eruptions, lions and tigers and bears, oh my! The list of major disasters that could strike at any moment is quite long and seems to be getting longer each day. Recently, the television has shown us more possibilities: super storms, asteroids, solar storms, rising sea levels, and global warming.

These are just the natural disasters that could befall the human race. We must also consider the man-made disasters such as terrorist attacks, economic collapse, runaway government, biological warfare, a well-placed EMP, wars and infrastructure failures. Additionally, there are disasters of a personal nature: job loss, death of a loved one, unexpected medical or dental bills, or divorce.

It is no wonder that many people are overwhelmed by the seemingly impossible task of preparing their families for disaster. If one tried to prepare for every single disaster scenario, it would not only be overwhelming, it would be nearly impossible…and very expensive!

However, as we develop a basic understanding of preparing for disaster, we discover a common thread. Basic preparedness, like a good coat, can cover a multitude of sins...or in our case, a multitude of disasters.

## Three Types of Disasters

There are basically three types of disasters: short-term events lasting less than a couple of weeks, mid-term disasters whose duration is anywhere from several weeks to several months, and long-term calamities that last from many months to a year or more.

### Short-term: This Too Shall Pass.

Short-term events can be natural or man-made disasters that require immediate evacuation such as wildfires, chemical spills, flooding, acts of terrorism, or storms that cause damage to the home. Short-term events can also require one to shelter in place or be unable to leave the confines of their home for the duration of the event, such as during an ice storm or pandemic. In these situations, supplies must be able to be gathered quickly and transported, or the supplies on hand may be all one will have for the duration of the event.

### Mid-term: Up Close and Very Personal

Mid-term disasters may involve personal hard times caused by unemployment, personal financial difficulties, death of a spouse, or medical challenges. They may also be caused by natural or man-made disasters such as hurricanes, storms, power outages, civil unrest, riots, or acts of terrorism.

Personal hard times require frugality, since food and supplies are limited. They may be available but one doesn't have the funds or means to purchase them, or transportation difficulties may hamper delivery of goods to an affected area.

With natural or man-made disasters, victims may have access to their homes, but are without utilities, services or transportation. Or, as in the case of many during Hurricanes Katrina and Sandy, homes have been completely destroyed and victims are forced to seek shelter with friends or relatives out of the immediate area.

**Long-term:  This will Change Everything Forever.**

Long-term calamities create a 'new normal' and literally change the fabric of our lives.  These calamities are generally widespread catastrophes due to wars, severe drought, devastating storms, or extensive acts of terrorism.

In a long-term calamity, victims might be able to stay in their own homes, but food and supplies may not be available at any price, or are severely limited. Survival depends on ingenuity and supplies gathered prior to the disaster or items that can be homemade or home grown. An example would be the deprivations of the Great Depression or the shortages experienced during the Second World War.  These types of disasters could require us to remember the old adage:  use it up, wear it out; make it do, or do without.

### Prepare for One, Prepared for All

Obviously, there is much over-lapping of problems, their duration, and causes. However, while the events themselves may differ to the extreme, there are some basic, underlying principles that apply to all disasters. Hence my belief that if you fully prepare for your worst-case disaster, you are probably fairly well prepared for many different types of disasters. This belief makes preparedness far less overwhelming.

# A Throw-away Society

Unfortunately, we have become a 'paper-plate society.' By this, I mean that we tend to discard broken toys, appliances, and clothes rather than refurbish, repair, or mend them.  We simply go out and purchase new items. That is fine, I suppose, as long as life remains good, but it leaves us lacking in both knowledge and skills when disaster strikes.

For example, do you know how to patch a pair of jeans or remake a dress to fit a growing child? Or do you wonder which end of a needle to thread? Can you sharpen a knife, split firewood, or repair a flat tire on your bike? Do you have the supplies to do these tasks?

Do your children understand the words "thrift" or "frugal"? Frugality requires we live within our income and even put some cash away for the proverbial rainy day. It requires discipline and knowing the difference between needs and wants.

The old couplet, "Waste not, want not" should be remembered, especially when one desires to be prepared for emergencies.

As you develop your preparedness plans, consider recent disasters: 9/11, Hurricane Katrina, the tsunami in Japan, the eruption of Mount Pinatubo, the earthquake in Mexico City, and Hurricane Sandy.

How long did it take for help to arrive in the devastated areas? How many days or weeks before basic services were restored? Did life return to normal…or was a new normal created?

## Planning is Critical

It would be lovely if I could look in a crystal ball and see exactly what was going to happen in the future. It would be so helpful in making life decisions. Will I avoid an accident if I stay off the freeway today? When should I schedule my Caribbean cruise in order to avoid bad weather? Should I date that charming fellow…or run in the opposite direction?

Unfortunately, I've never found a crystal ball that actually works. Therefore, I choose to live life to the fullest now and to prepare to the fullest for whatever may come my way tomorrow.

Being truly prepared means that you are prepared to deal with whatever emergency may present itself, by developing the proper attitude, learning a variety of skills, and gathering basic supplies.

The right attitude involves being willing to gain vital knowledge and skills before a crisis occurs. It means putting aside the negative comments about "those crazies who are into preparing" and set about doing just that…preparing.

Just as it is too late to gather supplies after the need arises, it is also too late to try to develop the necessary skills in the middle of the crisis. Can you imagine trying to read the instructions on how to fill a kerosene lamp in the midst of a hurricane? I don't think so. An emergency is not the time for on-the-job training.

## Why Gather Critical Supplies

"Why," you ask, "is it important to gather supplies? There are multiple stores within the radius of a few miles that offer every necessity and convenience known to man. There are restaurants galore from which I can purchase tempting snacks or full meals. So why do I need to store extra supplies? What could possibly happen?"

Let's examine Vicki's story.

Vicki was a serious, no-nonsense lady. However, she had a way of describing her experiences that reduced everyone within earshot to hysterics. She didn't intend to be funny and never understood why she was considered quite a comedian.

On August 11, 1965, a routine traffic stop in South Central Los Angeles resulted in a riot that lasted for six days, leaving thirty-four dead, over a thousand injured, nearly 4,000 arrested and hundreds of buildings destroyed… the infamous Watts Riot.

Vicki lived less than thirty miles from Watts. When she learned of the disturbance, she made a dash to the grocery store to stock up on necessities 'just in case'. Now, Vicki really liked tuna, but not just any tuna. She would only eat the expensive stuff: white, chunk, albacore. Later that day she called me in tears.

She had arrived at the store only thirty minutes after the riot had begun and found the store shelves nearly empty. People were literally fighting over what little remained.

"There wasn't any of my tuna," she whined. 'There wasn't any tuna at all. All I could find with tuna in it was <u>cat food</u>!"

At the time, her story struck me as hilarious. After all, it wasn't a life-or-death situation. It was just tuna. However, now that I'm older and, hopefully, wiser, the tale is no longer so funny.

How would you feel if you rushed to the grocery store for desperately needed supplies only to find the shelves virtually empty? What if you had a family to feed, children who needed regular nourishment? What would you do? I can almost hear you saying, "But that couldn't happen here in my home town."

Why couldn't it? It wouldn't take much to interrupt the flow of supplies: flooding, volcanic eruption, earthquakes or ice storms could stop all traffic on the freeways. Terrorist attacks, infrastructure collapse or labor strikes could also stop the distribution of goods.

Years ago, grocery stores maintained warehouses from which they stocked their shelves. Then the 'Just in Time' inventory system was created. Now trucks pull up nightly behind the stores to replenish the stocks. There is virtually no on-site storage, no inventory safety net! What happens if trucks can't make their scheduled runs for whatever reason? Bottom line….empty shelves.

It's a scary proposition. Empty shelves equal panicked shoppers and chaos. So what is a prudent person to do to insure food in the pantry for the family? Plan… purchase… prepare!

 Store extra food you use daily/weekly so that in an emergency, you are not forced to rush out to grab whatever you can find.  Plan meals and then fill your freezer and pantry.  If finances are tight, at least buy one or two extra cans every time you shop; they will add up over time.

With a little planning and perseverance, you can have a safety net of supplies set aside. It's a great feeling to know you have emergency food on hand...especially if it includes several cans of tuna!

The trouble is this: you don't know what will happen or when it may happen. In today's society, the possibilities for disasters are huge. Everything is normal until suddenly, without much warning, nothing is normal. Life can change in a heartbeat…and one never knows which heartbeat!

Personally, in addition to the ills of society, terrorism, and governments gone amok, I literally live on multiple earthquake faults. There's an active volcano in my backyard which is known as "the most dangerous volcano in the continental U.S." and I'm surrounded by forests that could lay victim to wildfires. Additionally, I'm separated from the nearest town by an old and rather narrow bridge that spans a portion of Puget Sound.

Additional possible inconveniences include the fact that my electric power tends to go off with startling regularity due to wind, storms, or if someone sneezes too hard. I could also fall and break my hip which would effectively stop me from earning the monthly paycheck that keeps my bank balance from sinking into the bright red zone.

True, I don't need to deal with hurricanes or tornados (hopefully) and tsunamis are rare in this area. However, the bottom line is that there are lots of possibilities for disaster whereever you live.

Since we don't know what's in our future, we should prepare for the worst. That means we gather sufficient food, supplies, and necessary equipment and tools to be able to care for ourselves and our families for a substantial length of time.

There are some activities I recommend that are all-inclusive. It doesn't matter whether you are preparing for three days, three weeks, three months or longer, the preparations will be the same.

## What and Where of Planning

Become familiar with the following information. You will need to explain it to the rest of the family when you begin to develop a family plan.

In case of a major disaster such as an earthquake or major storm, there are facts to be faced. First, accept the fact that you are on your own. Authorities and first responders will not rush to your aid immediately. Roads may be blocked, chaos will reign, and others may take priority. So, you must immediately answer three questions.

- Where will you be?

- What will you do?

- What will you need with which to do it?

**Where will you be?**  There are only four places you and your family members will be: at home, in your car, at work or school, or all the other places such as church, the mall, at friends, etc. These places we'll deem as "other".

There are limited provisions that can be made for "other" places or even work and school. Most of the preparedness efforts will be concentrated on the home and the family cars.

**What will you do?**  There are only two options. You may stay where you are or you may leave and go somewhere else. Stay or go. This decision will require some assessment of your condition as well as consideration as to the season and weather, the time of day, and the distance to go to reach safety. Additionally, one must consider his/her physical condition, any obstacles between your current location and that where safety waits, and if there is any assistance available.

**What will you need to do it?**  What supplies are necessary to achieve your goal?  It may require some role playing to create a supply list.

Let's look at a couple of sample scenarios.

Scenario #1 Earthquake while on the freeway!

**Where am I?**  I'm in my car heading home from church when "the big one" hits. Cars go everywhere, my car is hit several times and the doors are buckled and my seat belt is stuck. I'm scratched, bruised, bleeding and scared half crazy, but mostly okay for the moment. It appears all other cars in the area are stopped, so I'm not concerned about being hit again. What will I do first?

**Access the situation**. Am I hurt? No, not really. Am I in danger? No. Should I get out of the car? I want to, but I'm stuck. How can I get out? What do I need? Oh, yes. I have a small device created to break the windshield, plus under my seat, I have a crowbar that will help me pull myself across the hood of my car. Attached to the seatbelt is a gizmo that will cut the strap. Whew. It's nice to be prepared.

Next I must evaluate my situation. I ask only two questions: **Do I stay or do I go?** I must consider the season and time of day. If it is late on a cold, wet, December day, I'll probably opt to stay in my car until morning. If it's a lovely June morning, I'll probably try to walk home.

I need to assess my physical situation. Am I hurt of just shaken? Am I physically able to walk the ten miles necessary to reach my home? Would help arrive in due time if I stay in my car? Or am I completely on my own?

Other consideration in deciding whether to 'stay or go' is what obstacles are between me and my home. There's one overpass and one bridge between me and my objective. Will they be operable? Is there a way to navigate around the obstacles? Yes for the overpass, no for the bridge. However, I do know people with boats who live by the bridge. Hmmm. Is that an option?

Next, **what do I need?** If I choose to stay in my car, I'll need first aid kit, something to eat, to drink, and perhaps a way to keep warm. I'd like comfort items such as a pillow and some chocolate or lemon drops. If I'm going to be stuck in the car for long, what food and water is available? What about required medications? What do I need to be safe, warm, and comfortable?

If I decide to go, I'll need good walking shoes or boots and a change of clothes. I'm coming from church and high heels are not good for walking eight feet, let alone eight miles!

I'd also like a flashlight and perhaps a backpack containing other nice-to-have items such as those mentioned on most 72 hour kit lists: water, a first aid kit, and perhaps a small survival knife. I also need to ask questions such as these: How long will it take me to walk home? Will I need to camp out part way? If so, what supplies do I need and how am I going to carry them?

## Scenario #2   Earthquake in the middle of the night!

**Where am I?** I'm in my bed, sleeping in my worn but treasured flannel nightgown when an earthquake hits. My house shakes violently, windows are breaking, and everything that was <u>up</u> is coming <u>down</u>.

**What will I do?** I cower in a ball, protecting my head with my arms and pillow. My instinct is to flee the house before it falls on my head, but I know that trying to escape while the shaking continues is both futile and dangerous. I wait for the shaking to stop, knowing that aftershocks are expected. There will be perhaps only a few minutes where I can escape.

**Stay or go?** I will opt to go…to get out of my house…at least initially. Until it can be determined that my house isn't in danger of collapsing, I want to be outside. However, I don't want to be standing outside barefooted and in a torn and bedraggled nightgown. Therefore, I have placed by my headboard a 'bed bag' which contains everything I need for the first ten minutes after a disaster. I simply grab the bag and flee the house. When I'm safe outside, I'll dress in the weather-appropriate clothes contained in the bag. Also in the bag is a hard hat, goggles, knife, tube tent, lantern, poncho, umbrella, boots, socks, gloves, and of course, water and lemon drops.

Suppose I'm stuck? Suppose timbers or trees have fallen and trapped me in my bed? The bed bag contains items to help me survive: whistle, flashlight, dust mask, water, high energy food bars, plus other items previously mentioned. Since it's tied to the headboard, it hopefully will be within reach.

## Summary

Where will you be, what will you do, and what will you need with which to do it? You must answer these questions for several different scenarios that fall within the 'possible disasters' for your area. Then, put together a good list of supplies you will need for each family member.

Don't worry if you can't do it all at once. A little preparedness is better than no preparedness at all.

Be prepared. Two little words but they are vitally important. My goal is to lead you, step-by-step, to create a bare-bones-basic, short-term plan for three days to three weeks. Completing the objectives listed in each of the following sections will help you become organized…and prepared!

So…let's get started!

When it starts raining, it's too late to build an ark.

Disasters don't send invitations two weeks in advance

# PART TWO – BARE-BONES BASICS

## Project #1: Planning for Family Safety

**Objective:** To form a family emergency plan that will help your family to protect themselves and cope with a disaster.

**Shopping list:**
> Three-ring binder
> Permanent marking pen
> Several spiral notebooks

**Action:**
1. Make a floor plan of your home including primary and secondary escape routes
2. Identify safe places to go in case of fire, earthquake, tornado, storms or flooding.
3. Practice fire, tornado, earthquake drills
4. Decide upon an out-of-town contact to call who will coordinate information with friends and family members.
5. Once the out-of-area contact has been selected, provide them with phone numbers and names of all family members for them to call in an emergency.
6. Begin creation of an emergency binder
7. Date perishable good with the permanent marking pen.
8. If possible, set aside $20 to use for emergencies. Add to this when possible.
9. Find out what kinds of disasters can happen in your specific area so as to focus your preparedness activities.
10. Check out websites like Ready Kids for methods to teach your children about what to do in an emergency.
11. Obtain up-to-date photos of each family member and put them in a Ziploc bag to be placed in your emergency kit. They will be used if you become separated during a disaster.
12. Prepare a personal information card for each family member.

13. If you have family members who have special needs, ensure those needs will be met by your emergency plan.

An earthquake strikes. A train derails with dangerous chemicals on-board. The tornado warning siren goes off. Dad's at the office, the kiddies are at school, Mom's somewhere in-between. Cell phone service is overwhelmed. How do gather your family to safety?

It's the middle of the night and the smoke alarm suddenly goes off. Does your family know what to do? Do they know what <u>not</u> to do?

The unexpected can be very frightening. Family emergency planning is the key to surviving a crisis. If you have plans in place…plans that you have discussed and practiced… they will help alleviate fear and turn confusion and chaos into coordinated action…action that may save a life.

The first priority in becoming prepared is to develop an individualized family disaster plan. There are strategies to be created that will help you and your family prepare for the most common types of emergencies. By creating some basic plans, you will discover that you and your family are better prepared when the unexpected strikes. After all, knowing both what to do and what <u>not</u> to do in a disaster are the keys to survival.

Involve the entire family, including the little ones, in the development of your family plan. You want them actively involved in both the planning and the implementation process. Be receptive to their ideas and suggestions so as to truly make it a family project. Being an active part of the planning enables the family to cope better with disaster and to work together as a team.

**Plan a Meeting**

First, set a time for your meeting when disruptions will be at a minimum. The frequency of the meetings will depend upon interest, availability of family members, as well as the urgency with which the subject is addressed.

Create an agenda for your meetings. A basic outline might be as follows: Minutes from previous meeting, reports assigned at previous meeting, current objective or topic to be discussed, suggestions and comments, an activity, and most importantly, <u>refreshments.</u>

During your first meeting, select a secretary to take notes, give reports, and to assist in the creation of a three-ring binder that will eventually contain important information and forms.

Keep the meetings short and to-the-point. When discussing possible problems, don't get so 'doom and gloomy' that you scare your children or spouse. Keep it light, be calm and matter-of-fact. Emphasize that preparedness helps the family to cope with difficult situations and sometimes will allow the family to avoid those situations altogether.

**Plan, practice, and purchase necessary supplies: this is your best defense against any emergency.**

Here are some simple steps to take to prepare your family for emergencies. Adapt them to suit your individual family's circumstances.

1. <u>Involve each family member in the planning process</u>. This will encourage all to participate more fully in the planning…and execution…process. Even small children should have an opportunity to make their comments and observations.

2. <u>Set a time aside for family planning</u>. Make sure there will be no interruptions so that you will have time to complete your first objectives. This may be a challenge, especially if teenagers are involved. However, at least try to find a minimum of thirty minutes of uninterrupted time. Unplug all electronic devices, silence the phones, and encourage the entire family to focus on the task at hand: preparedness.

3. <u>Choose a family member to create a record of the family planning sessions.</u>  A loose-leaf binder may be appropriate as checklists, maps, and drawings can be easily added. If the person is computer-literate, he/she may prefer to create records on the computer. Either way, make

sure good records are kept. It will facilitate the formation of a "Family Emergency Plan Binder" at a later date.

4. <u>Discuss with your family the types of events that 'could' happen in your area</u>. In the Pacific Northwest, earthquakes are a major concern. In Illinois, tornados are more frequent, while wildfires are a concern in Colorado. Discuss the events that are most likely to occur in your area. However, be aware that no place in the United States or Canada is immune to earthquakes. Maybe they are not as likely in some areas, but there is always the possibility. Unexpected things can happen. I never thought of tornados (twisters) as a threat in downtown Salt Lake City, but one did occur a while back …and caused quite a lot of damage.

Natural disasters include earthquakes, floods, blizzards, ice storms, tsunamis, volcanic eruptions, hurricanes and coastal storms, tornadoes, wildfire and droughts.

Unnatural disasters include hazardous material accidents, economic and infrastructure failure, trucking strikes that disrupt the flow of goods, including foods, to markets, riots, and terrorist attacks.

You may or may not wish to discuss the possibilities of personal disasters as well. Divorce, death of a family member, major health issues, loss of a job or income may require family planning as well.

With the exception of earthquakes, most disasters give warning which allows us to gather our families, supplies, and our wits about us. It is my opinion, therefore, that if we prepare for an unexpected earthquake, we are generally better prepared for any other disaster that might occur as well. Therefore, I suggest planning for the 'worst case scenario' of an earthquake, then everything else will fall into place. Remember, there is no place in the world that is totally immune to earthquakes; some places they are simply more prevalent.

However, if you live in an area where tornados or hurricanes are common, you may wish to consider those as your worst case scenario instead.

5. <u>Discuss the places you and your family might be when an event occurs</u>. There are really only four places you or your family members might be: home, school or work, in the car, and every other place such as church, soccer practice, movie theatre, the mall, a friend's house, etc. In planning for an emergency, consider first the places where you are most often.

6. <u>Choose two places to meet family members: one close by and one outside your neighborhood.</u> If an event occurs when all family members are home, you will wish to select an outside meeting place. If a house fire is the problem, designate a safe spot for all family members to gather nearby. Even if a family member is visiting a neighbor, he/she will know to meet up at the selected location.

If an event occurs when family members are separated, select two locations outside your neighborhood in case you can't get to your home. Although it is probable that members will be scattered, knowing the plan will make reconnecting easier. For example, if your fifth grader knows that if an earthquake occurs during school hours, he/she is to stay with the teachers until a pre-selected person comes to get him/her. If your wife and children are at the mall, they know they are to assemble at a particular spot to meet up with dad as he makes his way from work to that spot.

Create a map of your area and clearly mark the gathering places. Try to consider all possible scenarios

7. <u>Select an out-of-state friend of family member to be your families "Contact Person"</u>
For a variety of reasons, during an emergency, long distance phone calls may go through where local calls won't. Select an out-of-the-area person as a contact person. Each family member will call the contact person, who then can relay messages to others.

Be aware that cell phones may not work during a disaster, but often text messages will get through. This is because text messages take less energy than voice communications. In the event that neither phones nor cell phones work, remember that in an emergency, ham radio operators may be able to get messages to loved ones.

Your contacts should live a sufficient distance away that it is unlikely they would be affected by the same emergency. Family members must be instructed to call the contact person to report their location and their situation in the even they cannot reach each other.

Additionally, provide your contact person with each family member's name and number so he/she can keep others posted as the current situation of each.

8. Create a "contact form" for each family member. Encourage each family member to memorize the contact person's phone number. However, it is my experience that in stressful situations, people will forget numbers quite quickly. For this reason, it is suggested that each member carry a small card with important numbers listed. See the forms at the end of this section.

Additionally, program contact numbers, including both parents and the out-of-state contact person, into each cell phone under ICE. Emergency responders know this means "in case of emergency"…useful under many situations.

When my children were small, I was afraid they would forget the emergency numbers, so I wrote them in indelible ink on the inside of the tongue of every one of their shoes. This worked beautifully, except when we lived in Hawaii. There they wore flip-flops! No tongues!

9. If you have children in school, check with the school to review emergency plans. Most schools require pre-registration of anyone who is authorized to pick up your child. Without proper registration and identification, your eldest child may not be allowed collect the youngest. Make arrangements now to register anyone with whom you have made emergency plans.

10. Gather important telephone numbers to post in a conspicuous place. Include work and cell phone numbers, as well as other important relatives, neighbors, out-of-area contact people, church leaders, the babysitter, school numbers, and anyone else who may be important to your family. See the forms at the end of this chapter.

11. Determine the best escape routes from your home. Identify at least two separate exits from each bedroom and common area and then practice using them. It is important that you hold regular drills, as minds tend to go blank during an emergency. You want your escape plans to be so well practiced that the required actions become instinctive. During an emergency, the human mind tends to shut off and actions become instinctive. If you don't practice a drill until the action becomes instinctive, things might not go as you would hope.

When folks are under stress, rational thinking goes the way of the dodo bird. My friend Vicki once had to flee her Topanga Canyon home as a wildfire approached. She frantically stuffed "important stuff" into a suitcase before she fled. That evening she discovered she had "saved" two pillows and a cast iron fry pan. (Note: read article # 1 under "500 Words or Less"

Like I said, rational thinking disappears during stressful situations. This is why drills are important. Practice until the desired response is instinctive. That is the only way one is reasonably assured of performing properly during an emergency situation.

Suggestions:
- Make the family planning session interesting but not scary. Stress that the reason you plan ahead is so that if something happens, your family is prepared and therefore, less stressed.
- Knowing what to do in an emergency generates confidence. Emphasize to your family that planning is a way of making sure the family is as safe and comfortable as possible regardless of what may happen.
- Serve a dessert at the end of your family planning session. Dessert is always a good idea.

## Project #2:  Emergency Kits

**Objective:** To create a variety of basic kits to enable your family to be self-sufficient for a limited period of time regardless of where they may be during an emergency situation.

**Shopping list:**
> **For each family member:**  whistle, flashlight, small knife, solar blanket, dust mask, water bottle, water packets and/or water purification tablets, high energy food bars, bandana, hand sanitizer, fire starter, mess kit, and basic first aid materials. Begin purchasing.

**Action:**
1. Make a purse pack for each family member, fill with small supplies. (See list)
2. Attach whistle and flashlight to everything imaginable.
3. Discuss with your family the evacuation plan
4. Place Bug-Out-Bins near an emergency exit or in an area that is easy to access.

In previous pages, I spoke of the four 'places' one may be when disaster strikes: home, office or school, in the car, or at home. It is our goal to stock emergency supplies in each of these four places. Obviously, it will be easier to stock our home and car than the office than those multiple places that fall into the 'other' category. However, there are specific items that can be carried. Let's look at each location.

**Disaster at "other" locations – including church, the mall, movie theatres, restaurants, and so forth.**

When away from home, office or your car, you will be limited by simply what you carry in your purse, briefcase, or backpack. However, it is quite amazing what can be tucked into small places if one is determined to "be prepared." A few items are absolutely necessary; many more will be according to your personal preference.

## 1. Obtain the priority items: whistle, flashlight and knife

The first items to purchase should be several whistles, flashlights, and small knives. These items can be attached to a key ring, the zipper pull on a backpack or jacket, clipped to a belt loop, or on a lanyard where they are always accessible.

The flashlight and knife, obviously, will be useful in many 'normal' situations as well as during an emergency, but why do I suggest a whistle?

Well, consider the film, "The Titanic." It was re-released not too long ago, again giving us the opportunity to watch the sinking of the famous ship, this time in glorious 3D. It's a historical-disaster-adventure-mystery-chick flick ...what more could one want?

I've watched the film ka-zillion times, but recently something struck me. The beautiful heroine would have died of hypothermia in the cold, cruel sea if she hadn't been able to acquire a whistle. That would have ended the movie prematurely. However, a whistle ... and clever writers ... saved the day. Whew!

Hopefully, you will never be on a sinking cruise ship. Remember, however, that there is <u>no place</u> that is completely safe from earthquakes and/or other disasters. The chances are fairly high that at least some of you, dear readers, will experience a devastating event of some kind sometime in the not-too-distance future. I wish that weren't true, but unfortunately, the statistics are against us.

Imagine you are trapped in a partially destroyed building. The air is filled with choking debris. As you scream for help, your fragile lungs fill with toxic dust. Your vocal cords tighten, refuse to vibrate, and your voice weakens to a whisper. Unfortunately, emergency workers can't hear your whispers. You don't want to be wondering, "Can you hear me now?"

They probably will be able to hear a loud whistle. A whistle that produces a sound of about 120 decibels could be heard over the racket and roar of emergency vehicles, rescue equipment, and frantic survivors yelling for their loved ones. In that situation, a whistle could literally save your life.

I am a proud grandmother of one small, dark-haired boy. Because he is so precious, I've insisted that his mommy attach a whistle and a small flashlight to his school backpack. Inside, crammed between books and other little-boy items, is an emergency kit containing water packets, a solar blanket, dust mask, and several energy bars.

Although he doesn't live in earthquake country per se, it eases my mind to know that he always has these items handy and has been taught how to use them.

What about your cherished children? I recently asked a third grade class if anyone had a whistle or a flashlight in their backpacks. Only one child had a small flashlight. No one had a whistle.

Our children are precious and we need to plan for their safety. This is why I suggest you purchase a small flashlight and a whistle to attach to your children's school bags. I'd also be tickled pink if you'd go one step further and assemble a small emergency kit to tuck in their backpacks as well. Remember, however, that students are <u>not</u> allowed to bring any kind of knife to school.

Purchase multiple flashlights and whistles. Carry them on your key chain, in your purse or briefcase, and in the glove compartment of your car. That way, they'll be handy if … or when … a catastrophe occurs.

Three of anything is an international distress signal. Three blasts on a loud whistle is the best way to let others know help is needed. In the event of a disaster, it just might be the one item that saves a life. It certainly worked for that gal in the movie!

## 2. Create an EDC pack for each family member (EDC= Every Day Carry)

Now, imagine that you are at a movie theatre and disaster strikes which forces you to stay where you are for several hours or days. This could be an earthquake, a chemical spill, or an ice storm. What items could you carry with you that would be helpful?

An EDC pack is the stuff you never leave home without; the basic survival items that would be handy in any emergency situation. Everyone should carry a minimal amount of equipment and supplies on their person at all times.

I'm not saying you should constantly carry a big pack on your back. However, a few items can easily be stuffed into pockets, attached to a belt, or in a purse.

What you carry will depend upon where you're going, how long you'll be gone and what you'll be doing, but start with a flashlight, whistle, and small knife attached to your key ring.

I carry a small tote that has three compartments. Two provide space for normal items: my wallet, water bottle, notebook, snacks, and so forth.

The center compartment, however, contains my emergency supplies: a dust mask, whistle, dynamo flashlight, bandana, a paracord bracelet, and extra glasses.

There are also three purse packs I've made from a pot holders and zip-loc snack bags containing all sorts of necessities: fire starter, matches, band-aids, chapstick, heart meds, wet wipes, and more. Check this link for instructions on making a purse pack: http://emergencypreplady.com/403/

Fill your purse pack with practical items that would come in handy not only in an emergency but during everyday inconveniences as well. An ideal list of items may be found in the section labeled "Lists".

The goal is to carry basic items that are not easily available in a difficult situation; items that will allow you to deal temporarily with the most likely emergency scenarios.

Last fall, a friend and I went to the Puyallup Fair. I didn't want to carry my tote or wear a backpack, so opted for the next best solution: cargo pants. It's amazing how much can be tucked into all those lovely pockets. That day, I carried my don't-leave-home-without-it items: a folding Kershaw knife, Leatherman multi-tool, micro-light, whistle, a large red bandana, a white cotton handkerchief, cell phone, dust mask, a three-day supply of my heart meds, matches and tinder, a small bottle of hand sanitizer, several wet-wipes, and lemon drops. This constitutes my basic EDC.

Plan to carry the barest minimum of survival gear on a daily basis. Select supplies that will provide safety and comfort until other supplies can be obtained and of course, geared to the age of the carrier. You may be eternally grateful to have just those few EDC items if…or when…disaster strikes.

## 3.  Prepare disaster kits for office and school

Disasters can happen while family members are at the office, at school, or while commuting in someone else's car

Like the "other" places, it may be difficult to adequately stock supplies at school or the office, but there are items that should be considered. Students and workers alike should have a small stash of emergency supplies either at their desks, in cubbies, or in their lockers.

Keep a box, bin, or backpack containing emergency supplies nearby. Some schools don't allow back packs in the classrooms, so this may take some creativity. At work, try to designate a particular drawer or cubby for your e-prep materials. As with all emergency items, the closer the better!

Tape an additional whistle under your desk at work. If you need to take shelter under your desk during an earthquake or other disaster, it will be easily available. This also works for elementary school students if they stay in one classroom at a regular desk.

4.  Buy sufficient N95 Dust masks and Mylar blankets for each family member and each kit.

Keep a dust mask in your pack/purse or briefcase and in your desk. The reason is simple.  In an earthquake, everything that is up will come down. As a result, the air will be filled with debris and dust, making breathing difficult.

During earthquake drills, students and office personnel are instructed to get under their desks, cover their heads with their arms, thereby protecting their necks and head.  Unfortunately, most are generally not instructed to cover their nose and mouth as well.
This is a dangerous oversight, as inhaling dust and debris into their lungs can be deadly, especially for those with asthma or similar breathing problems.

Dust masks should be the N95 respirator mask which is designed for infection control in the health care industry. When properly worn, the mask will help minimize contamination by micro organisms exhaled by others, and will also limit the inhalation of dust and debris.

N95 masks are available individually at most home improvement stores but they are often on sale at online sites such as www.beprepared.com where one may purchase a box of 20 for less than $15.00.

Additional items to consider for your office/school pack include a filled water bottle, a small first aid kit, a couple of high energy food bars, and a Mylar emergency blanket.

While water bottles are easy to refill, it may be preferable to have sealed water packets to add to your emergency pack. These individual servings may be purchased at most survival stores. They are easy to tuck into small places and are packaged to be viable for many years.

Most emergency supply stores carry high-energy food bars that are geared to supply adequate nutrition for several days. Some…well, at least a few…are quite tasty.

I have an on-going love affair with Mylar blankets. They are very inexpensive and they are easily tucked into small places. They are lightweight, compact, and waterproof. The unique reflective material maintains up to 80% of your radiant body heat to help preserve crucial warmth. They are reasonably large...enough to cover from head to toe, yet fold up quite small. They are so small, I keep five in my van's glove box and still have room for all the other items normally crammed into that space.

I also keep several in my home. I live where the power goes out if someone sneezes too hard. The back of the house is heated by a pellet stove, which, of course, requires electrical power to run the auger and fan. I have a fireplace with an insert in the living room, but high ceilings and open floor plan do not equate to a warm room.

Last winter, I was simply too lazy to connect the generator for what I was sure would be only a few hours outage. I set up my tent before the fireplace and to channel the heat into the tent, constructed a tunnel of chairs covered with   yep   Mylar blankets. Admittedly, it was a bit jury-rigged, but it worked. I was toasty warm and cozy for the duration of the outage. I did make sure I had adequate ventilation, as even a small fireplace can emit toxic fumes. Mylar blankets are a boon to mankind....or to little old ladies like me!

Incidentally, I do have a carbon monoxide detector, which I kept nearby during the event...just in case!

5. If there is a commuter in your family, create a commuters emergency bag.

Ahh, the joys of sharing a ride: you can ride in the fast lane, you save on gasoline, and if it isn't your turn to drive, you may even grab a quick nap on the way to work. However, there is the other side of the coin. You can't pack much emergency gear in someone else's car.

If you are a commuter, select a small bag that is both inconspicuous and easy to carry. Fill the bag with basic emergency items that would comfort you should you become stranded. Most of these items we've mentioned previously: Mylar blankets, water, high-energy food bars, et cetera. Don't rely on the car's owner to provide emergency gear. That's your responsibility.

## Project #3: Take the kit idea one step further

**Objective:** create a 'bed bag' for each family member

**Shopping list:**
        See text or see List section under bed bags. It is best to develop your own, individualized list.

**Action:**
1.   Create a bed bag for each family member
2.   Practice 'grab and go' drills
3.   Tape windows near beds


## The Handy-Dandy Bed Bag

Imagine this scenario: It's the middle of the night in December. Naturally, it is raining and cold. You waken with a start to a rumbling sound that grows louder and louder. A rolling sensation starts gently, but within seconds, the shaking is so violent you can't stand. Chaos reigns. Windows are breaking, Aunt Nellie's antique china cabinet crashes to the floor, and the ceiling fan is swinging wildly.

You want to flee the house before it falls down, but it's cold and wet outside and you've been sleeping in your underwear. The floor is covered with broken glass and you are barefooted. What do you do?

Here's where your family planning allows you to come riding in like a cowboy on a white horse. You've been inspired to prepare for emergencies. Therefore, you have a 'bed bag' tied to the headboard of your bed! This bag contains all the items you need immediately in case of an earthquake. A slip-on pair of shoes sits atop your bag. You slip them on, grab the bag, gather the children (who have grabbed their bed bags as well) and immediately leave the house.

When you are safely outside, you quickly protect yourself from further danger and cold by putting on long pants, a long-sleeved shirt, heavy water-repellent jacket, warm hat, and work gloves. Now, you change your slip-on shoes for a sturdy pair of lace-up boots and warm socks.

Other items in the bag offer comfort: a bottle of water, some energy bars, a small first aid kit, flashlight and keys to the garden shed where other emergency equipment has been carefully stored.

You gather your family and once assured that all are safe, you give directions: "Everyone has their own bed bag. Get dressed. Junior, use your Boy Scout skills and the fire-starting materials we've stored behind the house and get a campfire going. Mom, we need some hot chocolate. Cooking pots are in the shed. I'll set up the tent."

If you have a locked shed, pin an extra set of keys to the inside of the bag. Under stress, you don't want to be searching for keys.

Always have a pair of slippers/shoes placed on top of the bed bag with the soles facing upward. This is to prevent the shoes from filling with glass from broken windows or falling vases.

Please note:  bed bags contain only what would be needed in the first few minutes after an emergency. They do not take the place of a 72-hour pack or bug-out bin.

There is a second reason for creating a bed bag for each family member. Often during an earthquake, people may become trapped in their homes or beds. The bed bag contains necessary items that will assist rescuers to find the trapped individual (whistle, flashlight) as well as items to provide comfort (water, energy bar, dust mask, etc.)

The key to surviving an earthquake and reducing your risk of injury lies in planning, preparing, and practicing what you and your family will do. With luck, you will never need to use your bed bag, but it's always better to be prepared!

While we're discussing earthquakes, let me tell you a quick story.  An acquaintance of mine was in the Loma Prieta earthquake of 1989. As the quake started, he looked at his bedroom windows just as they shattered. Small shards of glass flew at him with such force, his eyes were cut to shreds.  He is now permanently blind.

Most windows today are not as susceptible to shattering as older windows, but I'm not one to take chances.  I have used wide packing sticky tape to diagonally tape my bedroom windows.  Hopefully, in an earthquake, it would lessen the chance of window glass shards flying in all directions.

For the aesthetically minded, the tape barely shows behind the sheers.

1. <u>Create a bed bag for each family member</u>.  A bed bag can be easily made from one yard of heavy fabric such as denim and 1.5 yards of braided cord available at any hardware store.  A backpack, zippered satchel, or cloth grocery bag could also serve as a bed bag.

2. <u>Practice emergency drills</u>.  Train all family members to respond by grabbing their individual bed bags.

3. <u>Confirm that the items in the bags contain everything that might be needed in the first few minutes of a disaster:</u>  See complete suggestions under the topic, "Lists".

4. <u>Tape windows</u>…if you're so inclined.

# Project #4   72-Hour Kits and Bug-Out Bins

**Objective:** Create a 72-hour pack for each family member and a Bug-out bin for the family.

**Purchase**:  As needed

**Action:**

1. <u>Obtain packs to fit each family member</u>. Packs do not need to be expensive, but should be sturdy.  Consider the size in relationship to the wearer.  A small child cannot carry a 100 lb pack!
2. <u>Begin filling packs with supplies.</u>  Each pack should be individualized.  Also, only one of some items is necessary per family.  For example, an axe may be in the father's pack while a small cooking stove may be in the mother's. Single or elderly people may find that a pack on wheels will be more suitable.
3. <u>Prepare a bug-out bin</u>. Obtain a large plastic bin with a tight fitting cover for this purpose. Be sure to select a container than can easily be loaded into your car. You may need more than one if you have a large family.

This bin should contain essential food, water and supplies for a minimum of three days plus prescription medications and a few comfort items such as lemon drops or chocolate. Tape a list to the lid to remind you of other items to gather such as your laptop, phone charger, etc.

Keep the bin in a designated location and keep it ready in case you must leave the house quickly. Your bug-out bin should contain essentials to keep your family safe and reasonably comfortable for at least three weeks.

## 72-Hour Kits and Bug-Out Bins

Get Home Bags. 72-hour packs. Bug-out bins (BOB). Get-out-of-Dodge kits (GOOD). Which is what? Are they all the same....or different? What do you really need?

It's easy to become confused, but the bottom line is this: They are two different emergency kits for two vastly different scenarios.

### The 72-hour pack or Get Home Bag

Bear in mind that the idea of the 72-hour pack has changed drastically in the past few years. Originally, it was deemed plausible that within those magic 72 hours, emergency crews would swoop down to rescue everyone in need. Events such as Katrina and Sandy have proven this to be a fallacy. Currently, experts in emergency preparation state quite strongly that guaranteed assistance within a 3-day time frame is not realistic. However, we continue to call it the 72-hour pack even though it may contain supplies for a longer period of time.

Imagine you are away from home and a disaster strikes which forces you to leave your car. The 72-hour pack is your "gotta leave my car and walk to safety" kit. Its purpose is to provide the essentials necessary to survive 'on the road' for as long as necessary to reach safe haven. For this reason, this 72 hour pack should be kept in your car.

So, what items are necessities? This is really personal choice. If you understand why you are putting together a kit and what the scenarios are for which you are preparing, you'll put together your own personal list of necessities. Contrary to many commercial sites, there is no "one size fits all." This is why I don't generally recommend purchasing an "all-inclusive" 72-hour pack. These packs may contain many of the basics but will not suit your personal requirements.

Remember that this must be carried on your back in a worst-case scenario, so plan accordingly. Generally speaking, having less gear that you know how to use and can carry is better than having lots of fancy gear that you can't use and can't carry.

The five basic needs one must consider to survive an emergency situation are warmth, shelter, water and food, communication, and first aid. If you can carry more, you may include other nice-to-have items, but concentrate first on the basics.

The first item on your agenda is to choose a bag. It should be sufficiently rugged to withstand the rigors to which it may be subjected and easy to carry. While a child's school backpack may be used as a temporary container, I strongly urge you to look for something more substantial. It must be large enough to hold all the gear you wish to cram into it and must have a well-designed system of straps as well as a hip-belt so that the load will be properly distributed. A hip belt is a necessity, especially if you must travel a fairly long distance.

Once you have selected a bag, the next step is to plan the items you wish to stuff, pack, and/or attach to it. It may be tempting to take the easy way out and purchase a pre-made kit. Please don't do this. Commercial kits often contain items unnecessary for your specific area of lack others that may be critical. With careful thought and a bit of research, you can develop your own personalized list of necessities.

Think of the rule of threes: It takes about three hours to die without shelter or warmth if you are in a cold climate, about three days to die without water, and about three weeks to die without food. Think in terms of what you may encounter as to weather, rough terrain, etc.

Also, consider where you normally travel and how far you may be forced to walk.

## Clothing

Disasters don't give much warning, if any. Assume that you will not be wearing clothes suitable for leaving your car and walking an unknown distance. A complete change of clothing must be the first items for your pack. Consider selecting several layers for cold weather protection, depending upon the climate of your location. If you live in an area where it is often quite warm, include warm weather garments as well.

Shoes are critical. Most people, especially women, wear dress shoes to work that are virtually impossible to wear over rough terrain or for long periods of time. My dress shoes are great for walking from my car into church and back again, but any further than that....forget it! Choose shoes that are comfortable, durable, and if you live in cold climate, insulated and waterproof. Include a good pair of wool or synthetic socks, depending upon the temperature.

Include a hat, both for sun protection as well as for warmth. I suggest also tucking a bandana into your pack as one may be tied in a variety of configurations to protect head and neck. A sturdy belt will come in handy as it can carry a variety of items such as a sheathed knife, multi-tool, or cell-phone.

Include a good waterproof parka or at least a poncho. If you live in an area of cold or wet weather, this will be an important piece of clothing. In that case, include a wool cap to be worn under the parka. You may also wish to include some long underwear!

If you live in a tropical area, you must choose your clothing appropriately. Dress to prevent overheating as well as for protection from the sun. Remember, however, that even desert areas can become quite cold at night. Choose your clothing wisely.

### Shelter

Hopefully, you will be able to reach safety within a short period of time, but it is always wise to prepare for the worst while hoping for the best. While you may be able to utilize natural shelters such as caves or hollows under trees, it is best to carry a rudimentary shelter in your pack.

The easiest is an emergency 'pup' tent such as those sold by Emergency Essentials ( www.beprepared.com ). These 'tube tents' may be purchase for less than $5 and are adequate for brief periods of time. They also are light and don't take up much room.  Add to these, a couple of Mylar blankets that reflect 90% of body heat and perhaps a hooded poncho and the minimum needs will be met.

If you want to go one step further for more comfort, consider a bivouac sack. It's an outer bag that is designed for sleeping on the ground while keeping you warm and dry.

An ordinary tarp is a good item to carry as well, as it can be configured to provide shelter or can be used as a ground cloth. The key is to know how to rig it and having the necessary cords. For this reason, carry a good length of paracord which can be cut to fulfill this need.

Tips:  A clever young fellow who knew I don't like to wear bracelets made me a paracord bracelet to fit my ankle.  It's sufficiently discreet to wear even when "dressed up."

### Warmth

The ability to make fire is crucial. Even though you may be able to walk to safety within a short period of time, it is best to know how to make a fire and to have the necessary supplies in your pack "just in case" your trek takes longer than you anticipated.

A well-built fire will provide light and warmth, cook food, purify water, dry clothes, comfort the soul, and keep away things that go bump in the night. Unfortunately, making a fire isn't a matter of simply striking a match and holding it to a piece of wood. Often, available tinder is damp or green. Windy, cold, wet conditions can further complicate attempts to start a fire, as can exhausting, injury or inexperience.

Yes, it is possible to create fire by rubbing two sticks together, but do you really want to do this in a pouring rain when you're cold, frightened, and miserable? This is why I recommend your kit contain multiple ways to kind a blaze such as matches, lighters, and fire-steel. Another lovely item is "Fired-up Emergency Firestarter." It looks like small lava rocks, but it is a safe, simple, and quite versatile fire starter. Besides being water-repellent, it can be stored for about 30 years, which makes it great for stashing in your 72-hour packs

Matches are inexpensive, but have a shelf life of only several years, so they must be rotated. Old matches may not light, especially if they have been exposed to dampness. Even 'waterproof' matches may not light under very wet conditions. Try this: bundle several matches together, tie with cotton thread, then dip the entire bundle in melted paraffin or recycled candle wax. Carry several of these bundles in zip-lock bags. They are more efficient than a single match.

Butane lighters are handy and light weight, but their fuel has limited shelf life. They may leak and working parts may fail, so are only a short term solution for starting fires. Pack several but check them often. Flint and steel, or fire-steel, is almost a perfect fire starter. It can get soaking wet and still produce sparks. One fire-steel can light thousands of fires and has unlimited shelf life. They are available at most sports stores or online.

Fire-steels work best when you catch the produced sparks in some kind of dry, fuzzy material. Cotton ball fire starters work beautifully and can be easily made at home. Roll cotton balls in petroleum jelly until completely covered, then store in a zip-lock bag. When needed, loosely pull apart about three balls so air can flow freely, place them under dry kindling, then shower sparks from your fire-steel onto the cotton.

A homemade fire stick can help kindle a blaze even in soggy conditions. To make a fire stick, cut corrugated cardboard into six inch strips about two inches wide. Roll tightly and secure with cotton yarn, then submerge in melted wax. Make sure the wax permeates the cardboard. Let cool, then dip again. Two or three of these sticks will start a fire even with green wood.

Just because you carry fire starting materials does not mean your attempts will be successful. Gather the necessary materials and then practice until you become expert with each method. Building a fire is an extremely important survival skill and should be learned in advance…not during a disaster when stress levels are high. Remember, your ability to create fire may be a lifesaver during unexpected situations.

Last summer, I decided I needed to practice my fire-building skills. It was…. enlightening. Okay, perhaps frustrating is a better word for my experience. I tried multiple times to start a fire with just tinder and flint, but wasn't successful. Next, I tried using a lighter with tinder. That wasn't productive either. I finally succumbed to temptation and used the cotton balls I'd prepared earlier. Voila! Fire! Unfortunately, the weather during my trial was sunny, dry, and warm. I hate to think how I'd have felt if it was cold and raining.

People new to preparedness often concentrate on gathering an impressive array of gear rather than developing the skills needed to survive during a disaster. My suggestion is to purchase several different ways to create fire, then practice, practice, and practice some more until you are absolutely sure you can start a fire under the worst possible situations.

As I've mentioned before, the three most important words in emergency preparedness are plan, purchase, and practice.

**Water**

After shelter and warmth, the next priority is water. Unless you live in a desert region such as Arizona or Utah, water will be reasonably easy to obtain. However, it is important that you have some way to carry water with you and a way to purify it.

Generally speaking, most easily found water will be unsafe to drink as it is. There are multiple filters available commercially that are suitable for your 72-hour kit. I like the Katadyn bottle purifier, as it is sufficiently compact to fit in my pack and will provide sufficient filtered water until I can get home. It's easy to use as well. Just fill the bottle with water, drop in the purification system, and then drink from almost any water source.

I also recommend purchasing a few water pouches as well. These contain 4 ounces of pure water in easily transportable pouches that can easily be tucked in your kit. They generally have a shelf life of about four to five years. Consider also a Seychelle water filtration bottle that supplies drinkable water regardless of the quality of the source.

**Food**

There is a wide variety of high energy foods that can easily be tucked into your 72-hour kit. These include sport bars, meal replacement bars, military MRE's (if you don't mind the taste), and the old standby, trail mix. One may also carry a small supply of cheese and crackers, pre-mixed tuna, or beef jerky. The problem with carrying food in your 72-hour pack is two-fold. First is the shelf-life. Nuts particularly go rancid quickly. Chocolate melts in the summer heat, and some items simply lose all flavor. The second problem is critters. Yes, critters...as in mice.

In the past, I kept my emergency food supply in my pack which is kept in my van. I had neglected to rotate my supplies for some time, so during a sudden outburst of spring cleaning frenzy, I laboriously lugged my pack to the garage. It was an "eeau" moment. Mice had chewed large holes in my nice, reasonably new and rather expensive back pack and what food was left was mingled with mouse droppings!

I set traps in the van and did manage to catch a few mice (another eeau moment), but their productive rate was sufficient for them to keep well ahead of my efforts. I was never able to eliminate all the mice from my van. In desperation, I finally sold it. (Yes, I let the buyer know about the problem!) Now I keep my food stuffs in a metal tin separate from my pack. I figure if I need to leave the van, I'll simply add the metal tin to my pack.

One non-food item that is essential to your 72-hour pack is a small, stainless steel cooking pot. Even for short term problems, it is something one doesn't want to be without. Most light-weight backpacking cookware will not hold up long, so I prefer to raid the Goodwill for a suitable pot. To save space in my pack, I've discarded the handle as unnecessary. I do, however, have a small hot pad in my kit. In an emergency, one can make a tripod for the pot from 3 same-sized green stakes pounded into the ground over a small fire. At a minimum, it would allow you to boil water to use with those handy little apple cider or chocolate milk pouches you've tucked into your pack. Yum.

You may ask, "Why carry cooking utensils when I plan to be home in less than 24 hours?" Well, I carry them 'just in case' because I can't guarantee that I can get home in a few hours. Even if I'm only 10-15 miles from home, circumstances may require an overnight on the road. It's better to have more gear than needed than the other way around!

**Other Gear**

Once the basics are covered, there are other items you may wish to consider: chemical light sticks, toiletries, hand sanitizer, rain poncho, rope or paracord, toilet paper and a whistle that can be attached to the outside of your pack.

I suggest you never go anywhere without at least one good knife of high-quality steel. It can be a fixed blade or a folding knife, but should be able to keep razor-sharp edge. I like a fixed-blade Bowie knife with a five-inch blade, but it is an individual choice. Also, be aware that different states have different laws regarding the carrying of knives.

Additionally, purchase a good quality multi-tool. These generally contain a couple of knife blades, a saw blade, a file and rasp combination, and a pair of needle nose pliers, a variety of screwdrivers, a can opened and even a pair of scissors…definitely a handy gizmo.

I always carry multiple flashlights in my pack: one that is solar-charged, one that is hand cranked, and one that is battery operated. I do suggest LED bulbs for all flashlights…they last longer. A few extra batteries will also be a good addition to your basic pack. A radio will be valuable as well. It will advise you as to weather conditions as well as the extent of the disaster which forced you to leave your car in the first place.

A small stash of cash, including coins, may come in handy during an emergency as well. Remember, in some disasters, banks and ATMs will be closed or unavailable.

A basic first aid kit should be a part of your kit as well as any prescription medications without which you simply can't survive. Add to your first aid kit a few comfort items such as insect repellent, antibiotic ointment, and a small tube of sun block.

Of course, duct tape should be in every 72-hour pack. There are multiple uses of duct tape. For an extensive list, please see the appendix. Another item that should be added is identification papers. I'll discuss that later under the title, Family treasures.

**Bug Out Bin**

This is the kit to grab if you unexpectedly must leave your home. This may be due to events such as a wildfire, a nuclear attack nearby, a 9-point-awful earthquake, or a sudden attack of zombies. It's basically what you would grab if you suddenly had to leave your home <u>right now</u>.

It should contain items for basic needs: light, warmth, food, water, shelter, and first aid/medications, plus personal items, especially copies of vital records and a flash drive containing copies of treasured family photos, etc.

The bug-out bin contains approximately the same type of items as the 72-hour pack, but...well...better stuff. For example, the sleeping bag in the 72-hour pack is something that can be packaged in a book size packet, while the sleeping bag in the bug-out bin should be a well-constructed, full-sized bag.

My personal "B.O.B." consists of a large plastic bin that contains a larger, more expansive version of my 72-hour pack:  flashlights and lantern, 2-man all-season tent, sleeping bag and mat, small stove, cookware, emergency food for several days, warm clothes and boots. I also have copies of important papers and family pictures on a password protected flash drive, hard copies of documents to prove my identity, cash, personal items and medications, and, of course, lemon drops. It's my "gotta leave the house quickly, but I still want to be comfortable" kit.

I can throw the bin into my car and leave with only a moment's notice. If something prevented using my car, I can also put the bin in a garden cart and "get out of Dodge."

Both the 72-hour pack and the BOB may stand alone, but the two packs do compliment each other. If I were forced to shelter away from home for any length of time, I would hope to have both kits available.

As you gather gear, please carefully consider each item: how it will be used, if it can serve multiple purposes, and if it is indeed essential.  Some items you can buy inexpensively. Some, you want the best you can afford.

Prepare a "Bug-Out Bin" asap. Select a container that can easily be loaded into your car. You may need more than one if you have a large family. Place basic survival supplies into this container. Include prescription medications and a few comfort items such as lemon drops or chocolate. Store your BOB near an outside door where it can be grabbed quickly. Tape to the lid a list to remind you of other items to gather such as your laptop, phone charger, etc.

### Sleeping bags

For example, I suggest you purchase a good quality sleeping bag for each family member. A good sleeping bag will more efficiently maintain precious body heat. Choose one that can form a hood and has a draft tube along the zipper to prevent snags. Select a synthetic insulation rather than down. If a synthetic bag gets wet, it can be wrung out and it will still keep you reasonably warm. If down filling gets waterlogged, it stays wet and you'll be wretchedly cold. Don't skimp on your sleeping bag. It's your best defense against a cold and miserable night.

Parents, select bags that will zip together so you may tuck a child between you and your spouse.

A quality, self-inflating sleeping pad is absolutely essential. Ground cold will suck out all body heat right through the best sleeping bag. A Therma-rest pad is expensive, but worth every cent for the comfort and insulation it provides. However, if price is an issue, a simple closed cell foam pad will suffice. Avoid open-cell pads; they soak up water like a sponge.

### Tents

The tent for your 72-hour pack can be a simple plastic tube tent. The one for your bug-out bin should be at least a 3-season, well-constructed tent.

This is one of the most expensive items to purchase for your emergency kit, but it is critical. Select a free-standing dome tent that is constructed of good quality, breathable materials with a rain fly that extends from the apex almost to the ground.

Many tents sold by discount stores have only a small rain fly that indicates that the walls are made of mostly waterproof material. The human body expels nearly two quarts of water per day. That water vapor will condense on the walls of a non-breathable tent, creating a soggy environment.

Tents are advertised as two-man, four-man, et cetera. This is misleading; it is the maximum number that can sleep closely with no room for personal gear. Divide by two for a more realistic tent capacity.

If you are six feet tall, you will need at least seven feet in order to stretch out and not be crammed against the tent sides. One needs about two and one-half feet in width for sleeping. My two-man tent measures 5 feet by 7 feet. That doesn't leave much space for gear or for another person.

Avoid tents that are larger than 10 by 10. It will be difficult to find a smooth, level spot for the tent. Also, bigger tents are harder to keep warm on frosty days, are less stable in high winds and more difficult to set up.

There are many styles and shapes from which to choose, but insure the seams are reinforced with nylon tape and the zippers are made of a non-rusting material. Better tents use thicker fabric and rip-stop nylon, which insure a longer lasting tent.

All seams in a nylon tent must be waterproofed with a seam sealer, which is generally included. Set up the new tent, apply the sealer, and let dry before using it. This should be done yearly.

In my midnight musings, I wondered how to create a warm, cozy environment within my tent. I know cold comes up from the ground. How could I pad the floor of my tent to keep out the bitterness of a winter night?

Leaves? There aren't many left during mid-winter and what few might lay beneath my maple tree would be wet and half-decayed. Fir or pine needles? Rather poke-y! I have a blue tarp to form a base, but would that be sufficient? Probably not. A rug would be nice, but difficult to store in my shed as most don't fold well, and I might not have access to those inside the house.

I spend far more time in hardware stores than absolutely necessary. Recently, however, the time perusing the local Ace Hardware was well spent. Wandering down an out-of-my-way aisle, I found something very exciting, moving pads! These are actually thick, padded blankets a furniture mover might use to prevent damage to Aunt Nellie's lovely old piano or her antique china cabinet during a move from Oswego to Orlando.

These pads are the perfect item to cover the tent floor, keep out the cold and to create a cozy cushion for my tender toes. Yes, I bought two. Budgets are made to be blown, right?

Protect your tent floor by placing a heavy-duty tarp between your tent and the ground. It's easier to replace an inexpensive tarp than your tent.

It's tempting to put cost over comfort when creating your emergency kit as you hope you'll never have to use it. However, don't skimp when purchasing your tent, sleeping bags, and pads. These items are crucial to the survival of your family. There are other items on which you can economize but for shelter, go for the gold.

Purchase these critical items now (hopefully on sale) before they're urgently needed. Mother Nature rarely loses her cool on beautiful autumn days. She prefers to throw her hissy-fits in cold, wet, miserable weather.

## Project #5 Family Treasures and Important Documents: To safeguard family treasures, important documents, and personal identification papers.

**Purchase:** Multiple flash drives

**Action:** Copy all treasured photos, certificates, and important documents to password protected files on several flash drives or disks. Share with trusted relatives. (See below)

## Family Treasures

Emergency preparation starts with the question, "What would I do if....?" That question has become almost a mantra in my household. What would I do if...the economy crashed...we had a 7.9 earthquake...if an ice storm hit Gig Harbor...if an alien spaceship landed in my front yard? Well, maybe not the latter, but you get the idea.

So, what would you do if you had only a few minutes to flee your home for whatever reason: wildfire, earthquake, flooding or whatever? What would you grab? Your kids, of course. Pets, probably. You might concentrate on warm clothes, camping gear, and survival food. Would you remember to gather important document, family photos or treasured keepsakes? Or have the time? Probably not!

When folks are under stress, rational thinking goes the way of the dodo bird. Remember Vicki as she fled her Topanga Canyon home and the important stuff she saved? Two pillows and a cast iron fry pan do not count as important stuff! It would have been better had she saved her treasured photos or mementos of her son's theatrical career.

Therefore, this task is vital. Make copies of all your important documents such as marriage or divorce certificates, insurance papers, and birth and adoption records for your children, copies of all credit cards, driver's licenses, mortgage documents, wills and death records, etc. Put the hard copies in a binder and place it into your BOB so it won't be forgotten if you must flee your home. Also, scan the documents to several computer disks or flash drives then send the disks to trusted relatives out-of-state. If something happens, you have backup copies elsewhere!

Next, scan all family photos to a disk or flash drive, especially those old, irreplaceable ones of your now-grown up kiddies as they start their first day of school, your parents' wedding photo, and the photo of your Great-great-grandfather in his Civil War uniform. Make several duplicates of the disk and share them with your extended family. Your photos are then preserved in case of a disaster and other family members can enjoy them as well.

When faced with an emergency, these kinds of items can easily be overlooked. Yet, a few hours of preparation now will give you the peace of mind of knowing your treasured photos and important documents will be preserved no matter what happens!

Remember, avoid panic and pandemonium. Instead, plan, purchase and prepare.

For a "Just in Case" article on this subject, please read article "Protect family mementos: Buy a scanner" in the section, "500 Words or Less"

## Project #6   Prepping your car for emergencies

**Objective:** To prepare your car to function as a safe and comfortable place regardless of the situation.

**Purchase:** Create your individualized list

**Action – as follows:**

1. If you normally wear dress shoes to work, tuck a good pair of walking boots under your seat. A heavy coat, rain poncho, hat, gloves and an umbrella might come in handy as well. They would be invaluable if you had to walk to safety.
2. Consider what kinds of items you'd want if you were stranded far from home and had to spend the night in your car. Think basics: light, warmth, water, food, communication….and chocolate. Make a list then begin to assemble the items.

3. <u>For light, buy a flashlight or a small, battery operated lantern.</u> Don't forget extra batteries. I may be being redundant, but consider the 'shaker' or dynamo type flashlights that do not require batteries. Include a couple of flares for safety, some candles, a lighter, and some water-proof matches.

4. <u>For warmth, pack a couple of heavy blankets or a sleeping bag, a pillow, and a plastic tarp.</u>

5. <u>Keep a three-day supply of emergency food in your car at all times.</u> Make sure these items require no refrigeration or cooking such as protein/granola bars, trail mix, dried fruit, crackers, canned tuna, beans, and Vienna sausages. Avoid the "pop-top" cans that open without a can opener. They can open during storage and make a terrible gooey mess. I speak from experience!

Be careful what candy or gum to store. Mint gum makes everything smell and taste like mint; Jolly Ranchers melt into a sticky mess. Individually wrapped Life Savers work well, as do Lemon Heads (my favorite).

6. <u>Store at least one gallon of water in four separate containers, so if one breaks, you still have sufficient water.</u>

7. <u>Gather other items as space allows.</u> You may wish to include some equipment if space allows, such as a can opener, paper plates, utensils and perhaps a camp stove and a small pot. Do include items such as a shovel, axe, pocket knife, rope and of course, duct tape. A radio is very important along with extra batteries. I also recommend a hand-cranked phone charger/flashlight/radio as a 'back-up' gizmo.

8. <u>Create a personal care kit with items such as toothbrush and paste, hand sanitizer, soap, and lotion.</u> Include a basic first aid kit and over the counter medications such as aspirin, Tylenol, etc. Don't forget a stash of any prescription meds you can't live without.

9. <u>To save space, remove the center tube from a roll of toilet paper and flatten it to fit in a zip-lock bag.</u> Add several heavy duty garbage

bags and a bucket with a lid to your kit for personal needs...just in case.

10.  Purchase emergency tools for each vehicle such as a box cutter, crowbar, and fire extinguisher.

## What's in Your Car?

Most families spend an inordinate amount of time in the car. Unfortunately, it is also in the car that many people get into trouble. They have accidents of various sorts, run out of gas in awkward locations, become stranded due to flooding or storms, or simply get lost.

Additionally, the family car will be the means of escape if an event necessitates an evacuation. Therefore, it is prudent that your car be well prepared for emergencies. The size of your vehicle may dictate the size of your emergency packs, but there are some items that must take priority over sports equipment, huge speakers, or simply toys (for both kids and adults) that tend to wind up in family cars.

On Nov 23, 2010 the first severe winter storm blasted my neck-of-the-woods with snow, high winds, and whiteout conditions that snarled roadways, stranding some commuters for hours. Winds of 30 mph with stronger gusts and temperatures hovering in the 20s meant a wind chill factor in the low teens. For those stuck in their cars, it was a frightful and dangerous situation. Unfortunately, most were unprepared.

I spoke to several of these folks after the storm had abated. They told stories of being terribly cold, frightened, hungry, and miserable. As they spoke, I recalled the winter of 1985 when I had first moved to the mainland from Hawaii. There was a similar storm and I was stuck on the freeway between Seattle and Tacoma as traffic had come to a complete standstill. While many were bemoaning their lot, I was serving hot apple cider from the back of my van to those stranded nearby. I was prepared!

So, what's in your car? Are you ready for whatever unique challenges Mother Nature may throw at you? Consider the area in which you live. Do you have winter storms? Snow? Ice?

Perhaps you live in an area where summer spends the winter, but severe heat can be a problem during much of the year. In that case, having sufficient water as well as materials that can be used to create shade would be extremely important.

My son lives in Arizona. His work requires him to travel the length of the state on a regular basis, but he resists carrying much in the way in emergency supplies since his car is usually packed tight with materials for his work.

Out of a mother's desperation, I created a kit-in-a-can for him. I filled a #10 can with desert necessities that would allow him to make a solar still, provide shade, and basic necessities such as water pouches and food bars. I sealed the can (I borrowed the equipment from a local church cannery) and then taped a manual can opener to the outside with duct tape. He has agreed to keep the kit in his car since it is small and compact.

He did appreciate it… I think. He responded by saying, "Thank you for doing this for me, Ellen." Sarcastic or funny? I'm not sure! Regardless, he has the can in his car… that's what I wanted.

Remember, by planning ahead and preparing, you can minimize both the danger and the discomfort of being stranded!

What about emergencies other than weather related problems? You might need to be prepared to be an escape artist…like Harry Houdini.

Oh, yes, Harry Houdini. His name was a household word due to his sensational escape acts. He died before I was born, but his reputation lives on even today.

When I was young and foolish…as opposed to being old and foolish now…I was fascinated with Houdini and often tried to emulate him. I would bundle myself in cords, climb in a box, and then escape with appropriate fanfare. These escapades convinced my mother that her hopes of raising a prim and proper young lady were unrealistic.

It was all fun and games until, as a teen, I watched a car slide from the road and plunge into Lake Shasta in Northern California. I saw frightened faces as the car tipped beneath the water; I heard their frantic screams. They were rescued, but the memory of their fear gave new meaning to the word, trapped. To escape was no longer a game; it was survival.

Every year, six million people are trapped in their cars for one reason or another, two just in the last two weeks. Some escaped without serious injury; others, lacking Houdini's skill, did not.

I'm claustrophobic. My nightmare is being trapped in a small space, especially if it involves water. Therefore, I have repeatedly asked these questions: What would I do if my car suddenly plunged into icy water, the pressure preventing me from opening my car door? What if I was in an auto accident, my seatbelts jammed and I was unable to release them? What if…what if…?

Everyone should keep within easy reach a tool with which to cut a seatbelt and break a window or windshield. There are many types on the market. I have one, the Houdini Pro-Rescue Tool, which is an amazing small tool that incorporates a spring-loaded glass punch, a seatbelt cutter, a safety whistle, and an LED flashlight. This handy tool is available on many online sites.

There are other items that one should consider for the car as well. A tri-fold shovel may come in handy, as would 12-hour light sticks, jumper cables, tow ropes, a crowbar, extra belts and oils, and a revolving signal light than can plug into your cigarette lighter.

Ready-made auto emergency kits are available at hardware and auto supply stores, or online. One may also create a customized kit by purchasing individual items. It takes only a few minutes, some planning, and most of all, the determination to prepare for emergencies.

Are you prepared to assist those in need in the critical minutes after a freeway accident? Are you equipped to help yourself and your family in an auto-related crisis? If not, what are you going to do about it?

Ask the question: What would I do if….? Fill in the blanks with events that might happen or that have happened to others. Remember, the six million people who were trapped last year <u>didn't plan</u> on being in that situation. Don't play that "it can't happen to me" game. It can…and it might. If you're not Houdini, you must be prepared.

## The Bare-Bones Car List

Some of these priority items may need to be rotated regularly, while some may stay forever…or until needed.

1. <u>Seat belt cutter and tool with which to break the windshield or window.</u> In an accident, seat belts may jam and refuse to unbuckle. Doors may also buckle and be unable to be opened. One does not want to be trapped in a car.
2. <u>Small first aid kit</u>
3. <u>Water.</u> Lots of water.
4. <u>Emergency food</u> Stock foods that don't require cooking, such as high energy bars, fruit roll-ups, tuna, crackers with cheese, and chicken or beef jerky. Peanut butter is the best item for emergencies. It doesn't require cooking, tastes great, and has lots of calories. Incidentally, remember that salty or dried foods will increase your thirst. Make sure you have plenty of water available.
5. <u>Emergency blankets.</u> If you don't have room for regular blankets, at least tuck a few Mylar emergency blankets into your glove box.
6. <u>Purse pack with individualized items.</u> including any prescription medications needed
7. <u>Flashlight.</u> Carry extra batteries, or purchase a solar powered or hand-cranked light. Some flashlights today offer all three power methods. Make sure whatever flashlight you purchase uses LED lights. They last longer and use less power.

8. Emergency radio. Purchase a radio that offers several power options: batteries, wind-up or crank, and/or solar powered. Many today also have a cell phone charger attachment as well.
9. Emergency contact information
10. Car kit with jumper cables, flares and other items mentioned above.
11. Small gas can. If you run out of gas, one major problem is finding a gas can. I've found that a gas can purchased at Wal-Mart prior to an emergency is much less expensive than the same type of can purchased on the road when you've run out of fuel! Incidentally, please develop the habit of driving on the top half of your gas tank. Always refill your tank when it hits the halfway mark. Never drive on the bottom half. That's simply asking for trouble.

Note: water bottles degrade in heat, allowing chemicals from the plastic to contaminate the water. Best containers for water are those made of stainless steel. Food also deteriorates in the hot interior of a car, so these items must be rotated regularly.

# Project # 7   Preparing your home for disaster

**Objective:**  To make your home a place of refuge and safety.

**Action:**
1. Conduct a Home Hazard Hunt – correct problems as possible
2. Create a family evacuation plan – then practice it

**Prepping Your Home**

Our homes should be our refuge in troubled times; therefore I recommend a home hazard hunt for items that may cause problems even without a major disaster.

One very important activity, especially if you live in an older home, is to verify that your home complies with the latest residential building codes. These codes were created with a 'safety first' attitude and are designed to prevent an emergency situation from turning into a major disaster.

## Home Hazard Check

Next, perform a safety check of your home. Here are a few things to be considered.

1.  Where are the beds? Move beds out from under windows that may break during an earthquake or if a tree fell on the house.
2.  What is above the beds? Heavy objects on the wall, such as mirrors or framed pictures, will easily fall during an earthquake. Hang framed pictures from closed hooks so they can't bounce off. Ceiling lights and fans should be supported with a cable bolted to the ceiling joist with enough slack to allow it to sway but not fall on your head.
3.  Are there heavy lamps on the bedside table? They might fall over onto sleepers. Fasten them securely to tables (this can be done with museum wax) or replace them with light, non-breakable lamps.
4.  Are there hanging plants in heavy pots? These will sway and perhaps fall during an earthquake. Stabilize hanging plants by screwing the hanger firmly in a stud...not just into ceiling boards.
5.  What's on the shelves? Breakable or heavy objects on shelves should be attached with museum wax.

**A bit about museum wax.** Museum wax is an amazing material with multiple uses around the home. It is capable of anchoring collectibles and artifacts from falling and breaking and it keeps pictures on the wall secured and level. I really dislike having my framed pictures askew, so I use museum wax liberally. A word of caution: Home Depot sells two sizes of museum wax. One is a very small tube; the other is a 13 oz jar. The price difference is only a couple of dollars, yet the 13 oz jar will provide one with sufficient wax to secure nearly everything imaginable.

6.  How are the cabinet doors? Consider a cabinet with latching doors rather than with loose latches. Cabinets may swing open during a disaster causing the contents (such as fine glassware) to spill onto the floor. Replace magnetic push latches with the

'child proof' latches that will hold during an earthquake. It's a bit of an irritation to open a locked latch every time you wish to get into a cupboard, but it's much more of an irritation to find your fine dishes broken on the floor!

7. Do you store glass bottles in medicine cabinets? Put items stored in glass containers on the lower shelves or at the back of a cabinet. Remember, parents, if you move items to lower shelves, make sure you have child-proof latches!

8. Do you have pretty glass bottles around the bathtub? They might break.

9. Are there heavy objects next to the exits or escape routes from your house? Make sure exits will not be blocked.

10. Do you have tall, heavy furniture such as china cabinets that could easily fall over? If so, secure the tops of all top-heavy furniture to the wall, such as bookcases and file cabinets. Be sure to anchor to a stud, not just to the plasterboard. Flexible fasteners such as nylon straps allow tall items to sway without falling over.

11. What about heavy appliances such as refrigerators and water heaters? These should be attached to the studs in the walls. The water heater is the most unstable appliance in the home. It's heavy, tall, and therefore is likely to topple over. Strap the water heater in place with straps around both top and bottom. Use heavy gauge metal straps rather than plumber's tape and anchor the straps to studs in the wall. Loop the straps around the water heater one and a half times before anchoring it to the studs.

12. How are your windows? A major problem in an earthquake is shattered glass windows, which blow out, showering those within range with sharp glass fragments. Since it is expensive to replace glass with tempered or laminated glass, consider the cheaper alternative of safety film which generally costs less than $5 per square foot installed. Another even less expensive option is to use clear packing tape to tape windows. This isn't as esthetically pleasing, but hardly shows behind sheers or curtains and it could keep the glass from shattering.

13. Do you use air conditioners or swamp coolers? Verify they are well-braced to prevent falling.

14. What is the outside of your home like? Are exits clear? Do nearby trees have dead or diseased limbs that could fall and hurt someone? Are stairs in proper order? Think what might be an impediment if you had to leave your home in a hurry.

Remember, everything that is up will come down if shaken, stirred, or blown. Develop the talent of recognizing what items might be dangerous in a disaster and plan accordingly.

## Emergency evacuation plan

In any type of emergency, every second counts. It is critical that you and your family, even the littlest ones, be familiar with at least two exits from your home. This is especially important where fire is concerned.

Fire can be beneficial, even life saving in an emergency situation. It can also be extremely dangerous. Recently, I watched a DVD chronicling a house fire that was very informative, but quite frightening.

I once believed that in the event of a fire, I would have time to call the fire department, gather valuables, and grab family photos and a few irreplaceable items. Wrong!

I learned it takes less than four minutes for heat from a house fire to reach 1100°F. Death occurs when temperatures reach 212°F. Heat from the fire will spread to every room, even rooms not on fire, where temperatures quickly rise to over 300°, melting plastics and killing occupants.

Smoke can be so thick that rooms throughout the house will be completely dark, even in mid-day. It is easy to become disoriented and unable to find your way to safety.

When burning, plastics produce fumes and gases which make you sleepy, confused and disoriented thereby limiting your ability to think clearly. Additionally, these fumes don't smell, so if you're asleep, you won't notice them. In that situation, your life may depend upon a functioning smoke alarm.

You're thinking, "I don't have plastics in my house." I bet you do! Many everyday items are made now with plastics including carpets, furniture, curtains, upholstery, bedding and toys.

So, what should you do?

Create a family escape plan. Make a map of your home and include the following:
1. Label every exit, including doors, windows, and hallways.
2. In each room, label the primary exit (usually a door or hallway) and a second, back-up exit (usually a window) in case the primary exit is blocked by smoke or flames.
3. Label every room where a family member sleeps.
4. Label the main shut-off valves for gas, electricity, and water lines. (More about this later)
5. Establish a safe meeting place outside your home where everyone can gather to count precious noses.
6. Instruct your family that they must not try to gather anything; their job is simply to get out of the house. Trust me; there simply isn't time to gather anything. If in doubt, refer back to the first part of this section. In less than four minutes, temperatures in interior rooms not on fire can reach 1100˚.
7. Instruct your family that if they are caught inside, to crawl or stay low, as the air nearest the floor will be less smoky
8. Teach your family how to use the back of their hand to test if a closed door is hot. It's better to burn the back of your hand than the palm; you may need the palm to turn a knob. Instruct your family to never open a hot door.
9. Practice the drill, stop, drop, and roll, if clothes catch on fire.
10. Practice your emergency evacuation plan….repeatedly. Practice on a regular basis to ensure all family members, especially the littlest ones, are familiar with all aspects of the drill.

Involve everyone in your home hazard check and in the development of your emergency escape plans. It is important that everyone in the family knows exactly what to do and where to go during an emergency. Teach your children how to escape out the windows in case the door isn't a viable exit. If you have a second story home, a good fire escape ladder is essential. Consider where furniture is located in each bedroom. You may wish to arrange the furniture so a dresser or nightstand is under the window to make it easier to escape.

A smoke alarm is a necessity. Place the smoke alarm just outside the sleeping areas, preferably on the ceiling at least six inches from the wall and at least two feet from any corner. Avoid installing your alarm near air vents, bathrooms, cooking stoves or any other drafty or moist areas. You don't want your alarm to go off every time you take a shower.

Test your smoke alarm monthly; dust it at least every six months. Consider a system that is monitored and maintained by an outside company. Consider purchasing a carbon monoxide detector as well.

Place your bug-out bins strategically near an exit so they are easy to grab in a hurry. As you perform your family drills, assign specific family members to be in charge of getting the bug-out bins.

Time your practice drills. See exactly how long it takes your family to gather safely at the gathering place. Remember that in a real emergency, the mind will often refuse to function. There is safety in a 'conditioned response'. In other words, life-saving actions will become automatic if one has practiced sufficiently.

## Utility shut-offs

Do you have natural gas in your home? If so, it is critical that you and your household members know how to shut off the natural gas. It is a well-known fact that after a disaster, a significant number of fires are started due to natural gas leaks and explosions.

Different areas require different types of tools with which to turn off the gas, so it is necessary that you check with your local utility company to discover exactly what type of tool is required by your system. Ask them for guidance on preparations necessary for your gas appliances and gas service to your home.

Learn the proper procedure for your particular system, and then share the information with the rest of your household.

Do <u>NOT</u> actually turn the gas off during a practice session. You will not be able to turn the gas back on, but must wait for an employee of the utility company to come to reinstate the service. <u>NEVER</u> try to restart the gas yourself.

Here's the rule: If you smell gas or hear a hissing sound, open a window and get everyone out of the house as quickly as possible. If possible, turn the gas off using the outside main valve and then call the gas company from a neighbor's home. Do not re-enter the house.

Verify that all household members also know where and how to shut off the water main that enters the house as well. There are generally two valves: one usually in the garage that shuts the water off to the house and one near the road that shuts the water off to the entire property. These also often require special tools, so check now and secure the proper tools. You don't want to be thinking, "Oh, my house is flooding…I'd better run to the hardware store and get a wrench." Aaagh.

## Security

Let's talk a bit about zombies. Most reasonable adults admit that zombies aren't real. However, the walking dead have invaded our communal consciousness, fueled by films, TV, and sci-fi novels. Recently, perhaps with tongue in cheek, some clever entrepreneurs have declared May to be Zombie Awareness Month. The festivities include an in-depth discussion of commercial products needed to survive the Zombie Apocalypse.

I happen to believe in Zombies…but not the lumbering, drooling ghouls so often portrayed in horror films. That's way too Hollywood for me! The zombies that haunt my dreams are those scary characters who, after a major disaster, emerge from the darkness to prey on unsuspecting neighbors. You may call them beggars, robbers, or looters. I call them zombies. Unfortunately, they live among us today, waiting and watching.

Imagine this: a disaster of Biblical proportions strikes our neck-of-the-woods. Power is off, bridges are down, grocery stores sport empty shelves, and people are without the necessities of life. Enter the zombies.

First are those who scoffed and teased you incessantly about being a prepper. However, when streets are over-run with desperate folks and stores have been ransacked, they will prey on your goodness.

"But my children are hungry. You certainly don't want my children to starve, do you? You have stuff, I know. You gotta share!"
They didn't bother to prepare but now feel entitled to your carefully gathered supplies. These are the whining zombies!

While you may feel like saying, "Frankly, Scarlet…", you probably will relent and give them a little something from your stores, but the time will come when you won't be able to without reducing what you have for your own family. Hard choices… whining zombies!

Next are those 'really nice neighbors' who ignored the hassle of preparedness. They even disregarded FEMA's suggestion to store three days worth of emergency food and water as a bare minimum. They considered selling their jet skis to invest in emergency supplies, but that was just too much to ask. Normally, they wouldn't consider stealing but their families are hungry, thirsty and frightened. They will do anything to provide for their family, even if it means pilfering all your supplies. These are the sneaky zombies.

Then there are the looter zombies. They figure a disaster is an opportunity to snag a big screen TV and iPods. They will riot in the streets to vent frustrations of an unfulfilled life or simply for the fun of it. After Katrina, New Orleans was filled with these kinds of zombies. Are there these kinds of zombies in our state? Yep. Could they spill over into our neighborhood? Oh, yes!

The worst zombies of all are the zombie-gangs. After they loot the stores of all electronic items to sell on the black market, it finally hits their mushy brains that emergency items such as food, clean water, lanterns, candles, and gasoline for generators are in high demand. They will turn to private homes, farms, and outlying areas. They can't wait to take what they need, just for the sport of it. Their methods: do whatever necessary to get the stuff. Violence is the norm for these zombies.

What can you do about zombies? It's a good idea to consider who might be approaching your doorstep *before* trouble starts. After all, no one wants zombies in our homes. They smell, they drool, and they take our stuff.

Generally, burglar-type zombies want to steal something of value they can easily covert to cash. They are more bold than smart and prefer to enter a residence when no one is home. 99% of burglaries happen in the daytime when owners are away.

Zombie-burglars like to work quickly. They want to be in and out before anyone can react. Therefore, my philosophy on home security is simple. Make your home a difficult, time-consuming target and the zombies might go somewhere else.

My home is a snug little cottage tucked away from the chaos and clatter of everyday life and I hope to keep it that way. One's home is one's castle, a place where one feels safe. Right? Unfortunately, nothing can destroy that feeling of security more than to discover your home has been burglarized.

Nationally, non-violent home invasions are on the rise. One California town recently stated that crimes of that nature would no longer be investigated due to a mandatory reduction of police officers. With the current economic situation, it's possible other cities may be forced to follow suit.

Fortunately, that isn't the case here in my area, but the story prompted me to assess security weaknesses and to minimize them. My goal was to make my home unappealing to a potential robber. Perhaps you should too.

Here are some basic tips to secure your home.

**Get smart.** Use the locks you already have. Many people don't bother to lock their doors when leaving "just for a few minutes." This is not wise. Lock your doors even if you're only going to be gone for a short time. Lock your front door and close the garage when you're working in the back yard. Burglars can walk in the front door, take what they want, and disappear before you've even know they've invaded your space.

Your home should appear occupied at all times. Use timers to switch lights and radios on and off when you're not home. Park your car inside the garage so thieves don't know your schedule.

**Get an alarm system.** If possible, invest in a monitored system. Apply alarm company stickers to all windows and place a sign near the front and back doors.

**Don't announce vacation plans on Facebook or post photos while still on holiday.** When going out-of-town, tell a few trusted neighbors and friends so they can keep an eye on your house. Letting the world know you're not home is an invitation to zombies to come a' calling.

**Make sure the exterior of your home is well lit and unobstructed.** Zombies prefer to work in the dark, especially if there are shrubs and trees that will hide their actions. Trim all shrubs and trees to leave a clear area of at least four feet from your house.

Flood lights, motion sensor lights, porch lights are all deterrents. Add additional lights to the darkest sides of your home, such as garden-style solar lights. Replace the light at your back door with a motion detector circuit.

**Strengthen your doors.** 85% of burglars enter through a door, so make it as difficult as possible for a zombie to get in. If doors and windows are locked, most thieves will kick in the door. Make that more challenging by upgrading the lock and reinforcing the strike plate. Purchase a KatyBar or DoorClub. Visit www.doorsecuritypro.com for additional ideas.

To help burglar-proof your home, install 1-inch throw deadbolt locks on all exterior doors. Remount the strike plates on all doors with 3-inch screws and replace any plastic window locks with metal locks.

Burglar-proof your glass patio doors by setting a pipe or metal bar in the middle bottom track of the door slide. The pipe should be the same length as the track. This also works for sliding windows.

**Strengthen your windows.** Window films such as Lexan polycarbonate can toughen glass, making it more difficult to break. This slows down intruders and forces them to create a racket trying to smash the glass. To keep windows from opening more than six inches, cut a wooden dowel six inches shorter than the height of each window. Drop the dowel into the metal gutter of the window frame so it can't be fully opened.

Personally, I dislike little windows that frame the front door. Although they allow one to see who's knocking, they also could be easily broken, allowing the robber to reach in and unlock the door. If you have those windows, either install a slide lock drilled into the floor that is out of reach from the window or secure the door with deadbolts that can only be opened with a key. Then don't keep the key in the lock!

**Get a dog (or pretend to).** A dog won't make your home impregnable, but it can make it look less approachable. You don't want a pooch? Post a "beware of dog" sign anyway.

**Be sneaky.** Door mats, flowerpots and fake rocks are the first places burglars look for your spare key. Instead, give it to a trusted neighbor or hide it in a place no one would think to look.

**Google 'home security.'** There are numerous sites with a wide variety of DYI ideas for securing your abode.

Most importantly, remember that a lackadaisical attitude may result in disaster. A door that could withstand the impact of a Mac truck is not secure if grandma forgets to lock it. The very best alarm system is of no use unless it is armed.

I challenge you to do something to improve your home's defenses or to make your home look like a harder target. Your goal would be to convince the robber to ignore your home and head somewhere else!

Prevention's the key to keeping zombies away.

## Project #8 - Strictly philosophy

**Objective:** To understand Normalcy Bias and to prevent it from causing problems.

## The Normalcy Bias

I'd like to discuss another phenomenon that concerns me. This is the 'normalcy bias."

According to Wikipedia … "the **normalcy bias**, or normality bias, refers to a mental state people enter when facing a disaster. It causes people to underestimate both the possibility of a disaster occurring and its possible effects.

The assumption that is made in the case of the normalcy bias is that since a disaster never has occurred then it never will occur. It also results in the inability of people to cope with a disaster once it occurs. People with a normalcy bias have difficulties reacting to something they have not experienced before. People also tend to interpret warnings in the most optimistic way possible, seizing on any ambiguities to infer a less serious situation.

The normalcy bias often results in unnecessary deaths in disaster situations. The lack of preparation for disasters often leads to inadequate shelter, supplies, and evacuation plans. Even when all these things are in place, individuals with a normalcy bias often refuse to leave their homes. Studies have shown that more than 70% of people check with others before deciding to evacuate.

The normalcy bias also causes people to drastically underestimate the effects of the disaster. Therefore, they think that everything will be all right, while information from the radio, television, or neighbors insist the opposite. This creates a cognitive dissonance that they then must work to eliminate. Some manage to eliminate it by refusing to believe new warnings coming in and refusing to evacuate (maintaining the normalcy bias), while others eliminate the dissonance by escaping the danger."

Whew! That's deep. Basically, the normalcy bias causes our brains to insist that all is well, even when it isn't. Obvious warning signs are then ignored. We expect life to go on as it always has and unfortunately, our brains are wired to accept that as fact. Our brain, in essence, says, "I can't believe this is happening. I won't believe this is happening. Okay, it isn't happening."

Let's look at a couple of examples. New Orleans before Hurricane Katrina is one example. Many citizens were in a state of denial and believed that the levees could never fail. As a result, thousands refused to evacuate. We know the result of those decisions!

Last year, numerous wildfires swept my neck-of-the-woods. The news was filled with photos of people standing like deer in the headlights, seeing the fires coming toward them and their houses, yet seemingly unable to move. They weren't packing their cars, they weren't gathering precious documents. Instead, they were in a state of total disbelief. This was the normalcy bias in action.

Understanding the normalcy bias will help one to overcome it when disaster strikes. Before an emergency occurs, condition yourself so as to avoid being immobilized by your uncomprehending brain.

First, acknowledge the uncertainly of our existence. Be proactive and do what you can to prepare for unexpected occurrences. Be realistic about life's challenges and what 'could' happen. The signs are all around us, even now. Look at the signs and project them into the future. That will clarify the things for which you might wish to plan.

Acknowledge your limitations. You can't do everything, but you can do a great deal if you put your mind to it.

Trust your instincts. When others are saying, "All is well" and your own five senses say otherwise, go with your gut!

Don't allow yourself to become overwhelmed with all the preparedness stuff that is hyped on the internet. Start where you are, make a list, and move slowly but surely towards your goal. Focus on what you will do this week or this month. Little by little, it will all come together. Also, remember, a little preparedness is better than no preparedness at all.

Make several plans: an evacuation plan and a hunker-down-stay-where-you-are plan. Make sure your plans are written down. Panic and stress tend to erase the logical thinking portion of our brains. Again, remember my friend Vicki and the 'important stuff' she saved during the Topanga Canyon fire? Two pillows and a cast iron fry pan. That's what stress does to our 'logical' brain!

It's better to over-prepare than to under-prepare. Don't let anyone belittle you into thinking you're over-preparing. Go ahead and get those extra cases of tuna or bottled water. Make plans that may be 'far out' but that are still within the realm of possibility.

Get physical. Physically fit, that is. Exercise is a good thing for both mind and body.

Of course, we can't prepare for everything! However, being a little bit prepared is a whole lot better than not being prepared at all. Being well prepared is even better! I'm not suggesting that you turn your home into a fortress nor that you become so obsessed with what "might" happen that you forget to enjoy living now. Instead, I hope you will learn the principles of preparedness and determine what will work for you and your family. Then just do it! Do what is necessary, one step at a time, with a personalized plan of action.

**Project #9** Food for your table

**Objective:** To gather sufficient food supplies to feed your family for up to three weeks

**Action:**
1. Create menus for three weeks of survival and comfort foods
2. Make a list of necessary supplies
3. As possible, create a stockpile of these foods
4. Remember to rotate your stockpile

# Food storage

Imagine this scenario: an earthquake has raised havoc in your town. Power lines are down, roads are blocked, and chaos reigns. Stores are closed; shelves are empty. Outside help is slow to arrive.

Tummies are growling, demanding food. Do you have sufficient food on hand to feed your family? If not, what will you do? Hopefully, you will be able turn to your emergency food storage supplies.

There are three levels of food storage: emergency, short term, and long term.

An emergency food storage program is geared to sustain your family during a crisis that may last from three days to three weeks. Short term is considered three weeks to three months, and long term is from three months to one year or more.

For our purposes, we will concentrate on the emergency level: food for three days to three weeks of a disaster.

During the first days of a disaster, individual stress levels are extremely high. It's difficult to focus on preparing comforting, healthy meals. Yet, that's exactly what's needed to restore a sense of normalcy, especially for children. The food stored for this very scary time should be items that are easy to fix, healthy, tasty, and most of all, familiar. It is <u>not</u> the time to introduce strange new foods.

My preference for the early days of a disaster are the "just add water" meals. Several companies offer a variety of entrees, side dishes, and even desserts. Add hot water; wait a few minutes, and voila! Dinner is ready.

Imagine: Loaded Scalloped Potatoes… thick slices of potato and savory bacon bits in a creamy cheddar sauce. Creamy Chicken Noodle Soup. Chili Lime Chicken and Rice. Sound good? Yes. Quick and easy to fix? Absolutely! These 'Thrive Express" items are available all over the U.S. and Canada via local distributors or you can connect with a distributor through my website, www.emergencypreplady.com

Mountain House meals are available at Wal-Mart in the camping section, at REI, or online.

These instant meals are the best option for the initial days of an emergency. Purchase enough to feed your family for at least the first week after a disaster when stress levels are high and uncomplicated cooking is a priority.

Next, create menus for breakfast, lunch, dinner, and snacks. For example, hot oatmeal with dried fruit for one breakfast, pancakes for the second, cold cereal for a third. Select lunches such as peanut butter and jelly sandwiches, macaroni and cheese, or chili beans. Plan lunches that your family enjoys and that are easy to prepare. Do the same for dinner. Try for as much variety as possible, but stay within foods that are familiar to your family and are easy to prepare.

After you have planned a menu that reflects your normal diet, likes and dislikes, purchase sufficient supplies to serve these meals for at least three weeks. Most of us can't purchase all these goods in one fell swoop. However, hopefully you can purchase a few extra items each week and gradually increase your stockpile until you have sufficient provisions for three weeks.

Once you have sufficient supplies, shop from your pantry and replace what you've used. This keeps your supplies rotated. Experiment with the instant meals so your family can discover which ones they enjoy and which one's simply don't work.

For example, I enjoy Thrive scalloped potatoes and their chicken soup is amazing. (Although I must admit, I add some canned chicken to the soup.) I don't care for Mountain House scrambled eggs and bacon (too smoky), but their Chili Mac and Cheese is quite tasty.

The goal is to have a three-week supply of basic meals that meet the "emergency" criteria: easy to fix, healthy, and comforting. You want to be able to say, "Don't worry, kiddos, we're okay. We have our emergency supply of food!"

Once you have the basics of your plan, try to add a little "sugar and spice" to the mix. Hot chocolate or apple cider mixes can be simply added to water for a warm, comforting drink. A bottle of "Tang" orange drink may be quite sugary, but will cover the taste of chemically purified water. Nuts, dried cranberries, and chocolate chips make a tasty trail mix. Hard candies store well and can be a wonderful morale builder during tough times.

Remember to rotate your food storage to avoid spoilage. These items generally are not packaged for long term storage. You can't just buy the items, stick them away somewhere and forget about them. The rule is "store what you eat and eat what you store.'

The ideal for a three-week food storage plan is one week of comfort food that is quick and easy to prepare, then two weeks of familiar foods that may take a bit more effort to prepare but offer a sense that things may be returning to normal. This is especially important when your family encompasses small children.

Now, if you are a single little old lady like me, three weeks of food won't take up much space. However, if you're providing for a young family with several children, you may wish to consider freeze dried and dehydrated foods for your three week supply.

Don't wrinkle up your nose! Whether you realize it or not, you probably use dehydrated foods on a regular basis. Think of those lovely blue boxes of macaroni and cheese. Dehydrated. The fruit in your Raisin Bran, that oh-so-convenient box of au gratin potatoes. Yep, also dehydrated.

So what is the difference between buying a box of au gratin potatoes or #10 cans of potato slices, cheese blend, and powdered milk? Many more servings, less expensive, longer shelf life…and just as tasty. And you get a bonus…it takes up less room.

I once helped prepare a 'survivor' dinner of lasagna with meat sauce, green beans with bacon, onions and mushrooms, fresh rolls, orange smoothies and a yummy peach cobbler. Everything was from dehydrated or freeze dried supplies including all the ingredients for the lasagna. (I made cottage cheese from powdered milk.) It was delicious and no one believed everything was from freeze-dried or dehydrated supplies. Yes, even the bacon!

It's amazing what's available in freeze-dried and dehydrated foods. The basics are dehydrated such as wheat and grains, white rice, beans, powdered milk, pasta, apple slices, potato flakes, chocolate pudding, onions, and sugar. Freeze dried items will add variety and tickle your taste buds: strawberries, bananas, corn, peas, green beans, spinach, celery and much more. These are packed for an extended shelf-life….up to 30 years!

Wal-Mart has a small selection of these items. Emergency Essentials at www.beprepared.com offers a whole range of foods and emergency supplies. Thrive is available in a variety of places including my website. They offer parties where participants can taste their products. Try the freeze-dried pineapple, raspberries, or mango. They're yummy!

The best idea is to purchase long-term storage foods, but use them in everyday cooking. That way, when disaster strikes, you know how to cook with dehydrated and freeze-dried foods.

With proper planning, one can develop a food storage plan with great menus that even the pickiest eaters will enjoy.

# Project #10   A major necessity: water

**Objective:** To store sufficient water for short-term use and learn methods of water purification for longer term emergencies.

**Action:**
1.   Decide upon which water storage system works best for you
2.   Start immediately to store water, if nothing more than filling a few empty juice containers with fresh water.
3.   Plan your water storage program then get started as finances allow.

**Gurgle, gurgle, gulp....got water?**

Congratulations! You've taken the series so far to heart and have started a food storage program. Feels great to be getting prepared for the unexpected, doesn't it? However, while you've been busy planning your food storage, you might have overlooked one essential item: Water.

It's easy to forget the need to store water. We're accustomed to having all the water we need, courtesy of public utilities. Yet, there are many circumstances that could disrupt the flow of water to your home. Avoid the tendency to think about water once your food storage is completely organized. You should plan your food and water supplies simultaneously.

Remember Coleridge's poem, <u>The Rime of the Ancient Mariner</u>? The Ancient Mariner is becalmed, stored water gone, the sea is salty and therefore unfit for consumption - thus his lament, "Water, water everywhere but not a drop to drink!"

If you do not have sufficient water storage and a way to replenish your stash, the lament of the Ancient Mariner may be yours as well.

**Why store water?**

It doesn't take much to stop that stream of clean water that flows magically from your tap. Perhaps you need to turn off your water due to a frozen pipe. A broken water main may cut off service to the entire neighborhood. The local water source may become polluted, or a natural disaster occurs that causes havoc and shuts down all city services…including water.

It really doesn't matter if your water is off for six hours, three days, or several weeks, being without a reliable source of water is distressing. A temporary shutoff is terribly inconvenient. Having the water supply shut off for weeks or more due to a major disaster isn't just inconvenient, it's disastrous.

Water is essential for all facets of life: for drinking, cooking, washing our dishes and clothes, and for personal hygiene. Here's something else many forget: it takes water to flush toilets. If water is shut off, you'll need a bucket of water handy to flush the toilet.

Every household should store some water for emergencies.

**How much water should be stored?**

In an emergency, you must have sufficient water on hand for drinking and cooking, and to flush toilets, wash clothes, and bathe. (I'm talking spit-baths here…not a long, luxurious hot shower.)

Even if you decide to forego showers for a day or two, you'll still need a <u>minimum</u> of one gallon of water per day per person. This allows each person two quarts for drinking and cooking and two quarts for washing. It may be a challenge to store a three-week supply or 21 gallons per person, yet this is the minimum recommended amount. If you have room, it would be wise to store a greater amount, especially if you're like me and can't endure two days without washing your hair.

For a personal, local, short term event, you may not need this much water. However, in that case, I'll bet some of your unprepared neighbors will be grateful for your foresightedness. In a major disaster, pure water will be in short supply. Therefore, it's prudent to store as much as your space allows.

You can count as part of that requirement bottled juice or even liquid from canned goods. There is usually about one cup of liquid in canned veggies that could be used in cooking. For example, cook your dry macaroni in juice from corn or peas.

## Water Collection

Unless you live in a castle with lots of storage room (which most of us don't), it is impossible to store vast amounts of water. It's heavy and it takes up a great deal of room. Therefore, the wise and prudent look for ways to replenish their supply.

I live in the Pacific Northwet....yes, the 's' was left out intentionally. Here people complain that it rains <u>13</u> months of the year. That isn't quite accurate...but sometimes it feels that way. In Western Washington, rains are plentiful. Therefore, I store as much water as possible but I also plan to replenish my supply by collecting of rain water.

For non-potable water for flushing toilets and washing, build a water catchment system. It's so easy, even a caveman... or this little old lady... could do it! Mine consists of two barrels, appropriate spouts and spigots, and a cute dragon gargoyle to add a bit of class to the system. The water is collected from the roof via the gutters which drain through a downspout and into the rain barrel.

Rain water can be filtered and purified for drinking and cooking purposes if you have the proper filters and purifying agents handy.

Is rain a potential source of water in your area? Should you have a way to collect rain water? Do you have a way of testing the water? Do you have a way to filter and purify it? These are questions that must be answered on an individual basis.

In a large scale disaster, water is easily contaminated. Drinking contaminated water can lead to nausea, cramping, headaches, vomiting and diarrhea. The associated dehydration can lead to death, especially in the elderly or infants.

There are three generally accepted methods of treating water for drinking and cooking plus two other methods that have just recently been offered. Boiling, filtering, chemical treatments are the standards. Ultraviolet radiation and the PUR clean drinking water kit are the recent additions.

### Boiling

Contrary to popular belief, it is not necessary to actually bring water to a full rolling boil or to boil for 5 to 10 minutes in order to sterilize the water. Heating the water to a temperature of 155` F (70`C) is sufficient to kill most of the creepy-crawlies. Since in a disaster setting, you may not have a thermometer with which to measure water temperature, the most practical approach is to heat the water until it starts bubbling.

Personally, I accept the advice of the Centers for Disease Control and Prevention (CDC) who recommends boiling water for one minute.

The advantages of boiling water are that it kills most micro organism, it's practical, and it doesn't take a rocket scientist to do it.

The disadvantages are that boiling does not remove silt, dust, or volcanic ash, it does not remove chemical contamination, and it requires fuel…fuel which in some circumstances may be difficult to obtain.

### Filtering

Filters function by forcing water through a medium with tiny holes to physically remove microbes and matter. Anything larger than the hole is blocked. Most good filters will remove parasites, bacteria and some viruses. Some use a chemical purifier such as iodine resin to kill viruses. Most purifiers must prove able to remove the basic biological contaminants (protozoa, bacteria, and viruses) to satisfy the EPA.

The advantages of filters are they are generally effective against bacteria and parasites, some filters remove larger viruses, and they are convenient, fast, and many will fit in your 72-hour pack or bug-out bin.

The major disadvantage is that if you are in an area where viral contamination is present (such as after a major disaster where sanitation is poor) additional purification by boiling or chemical treatment is still required.

**Chemical Treatment**

Chemical treatment is via chlorine or iodine. Both iodine and chlorine are very effective against most common pathogens, but be aware they do not act immediately but require sufficient time to do their job. This time also increases as the temperature decreases.

Iodine is most often used in the form of tablets. One or two tablets can be added to a liter of water and requires about 30 minutes at room temperature to be effective.

The advantage of iodine is that it is effective against most common pathogens and is faster than chlorine (30 minutes versus 4 hours).

The disadvantage of iodine is that it does not kill some parasites, does not remove chemical contaminates, and in temperatures below 70` F (20` C) it requires increasingly longer times in order to render the water potable.

Additionally, some people react badly to iodine and most medical personnel recommend not using iodine treated water longer than 3 to 4 weeks. Personally, I don't like the taste. To counteract this, I wait until the iodine has had plenty of time to work, then I add several spoonfuls of "Tang" or a similar product to mask the taste.

Chlorine can be purchased in the form of chlorine dioxide tablets or drops. One may also use laundry bleach but be sure it is pure. Do not use bleach that has added perfumes or other chemicals.

Chlorine will kill most bacteria and parasites in a few minutes, but giardia and cryptosporidium and other viruses require as much as four hours to be affected by the chlorine... and that's a room temperature. The time is longer in colder situations. Always follow the manufacturer's recommendations when using any purification method.

Unlike iodine, chlorine can be used indefinitely. However, chemical treatments do not remove chemical contaminants.

### Ultraviolet Radiation

A relative newcomer to techniques for purifying water is via ultraviolet radiation. The most common device is the SteriPen. It's a battery-operated gismo that is immersed in a one-liter, wide-mouth bottle for a couple of minutes. Cool, huh?

However, be aware that UV radiation doesn't remove chemical contaminants. Also, the water should be fairly clear...so if it's not, either allow it to settle or use a filter to remove most of the sediment. This is a good place to use those coffee filters you've been saving. They will filter out much of the sediment.

A SteriPen is a handy device that is fast and convenient, especially for tucking into your 72-hour pack. However, remember it does require batteries.

### PUR Water Treatment kit

PUR is a Swiss division of Proctor and Gamble. They created the water treatment kit for use in Third World countries, but it is now available in North America. The kit will purify water and remove biological and some chemical contaminants in about twenty minutes.

There are a few problems with the kit. It's a wee bit difficult to obtain, although it has gotten easier recently. What bothers me the most is that the packets are pre-measured for 10 liters and you can't use just half of a packet. It's basically all or nothing. This is a bit inconvenient for a small family…or for a single person like me!

However, it's reasonably inexpensive, easy to use, and quite effective.

### Bottom line

I firmly believe in that strange saying, "Two is one, one is none." Translated, that means you should always have a "Plan B"…and I recommend a plan C, D, and maybe even an E as well. Choose at least two ways of to guarantee that you have sufficient water for your needs.

### Water Storage Containers: Pros and Cons

It's important that stored water is kept clean and pure, so choosing the proper container is critical.

There are many different sizes and shapes of containers in which to store water, including used soda or juice bottles, 5-6 gallon jugs, Mylar lined boxes, water bricks, and large barrels. Each has some advantages and disadvantages.

Soda or juice bottles are free; however, it is virtually impossible to remove all traces of previous contents so one must be concerned about bacteria. Water stored in them must be disinfected or filtered prior to use.

5 or 6 gallon plastic jugs are convenient, manageable, and cost effective. Purchased new, these jugs can be used only for water, thereby eliminating the risks associated with using a "second-hand" container. However, they're heavy when filled and must be rotated yearly.

Mylar lined boxes are the best bet for those who would like to "store and forget" their water supply for several years. Mylar water boxes only need to be rotated once every five years. They also stack well, up to three boxes high, and are cost-effective, and can be slid under beds. However, they are rather complicate to set up and fill, are not very convenient for when an emergency necessitates using only a small amount of your water storage.

Relatively new in water storage programs, water bricks hold 3.5 gallons per brick, which makes them more manageable than either the 5-6 gallon containers or the big water barrels. They can also be stacked clear to the ceiling, thus saving lots of storage space and they are safe to freeze as long as you allow for head room. These require yearly rotation as well.

On the negative side, they are more expensive per gallon and not locally available, so add shipping charges to the price. They are best for people who have extra storage space and no budget restraints. Water bricks are extremely desirable and are on my wish list.

Water barrels are the best solution for storing lots of water. They are available in sizes from 30 to 250 gallons. Water barrels must be rotated once a year, but with additives, that can be extended to once every five years. There are setbacks, however. They are rather difficult to empty and rotate, as they require a hand pump. I suggest installing a faucet for this purpose. Always fill and empty the barrels with a food grade hose used only for that purpose. A hose left on the ground gathers creepy crawlies!

**Basic Tips**

Never use plastic milk cartons for water storage. They are not meant for secondary usage, probably will leak, and can harbor bacteria. Plastic juice bottles are not good for long term storage either. The bottles retain juice no matter how thoroughly they are washed, allowing bacteria to breed. One can purchase three-gallon bottles at stores such as "Water to Go". Refill as they are used so they are continually rotated.

Put bottles of water in the freezer to fill empty spaces. You will not only have extra water, it will help keep the freezer cold during power outages. Don't use milk jugs for this. They break too easily. Also, remember not to fill bottles to the top. You must allow for expansion.

55 gallon barrels are available both new and used. If you purchase used barrels, don't buy ones previously used for soy sauce. You'll <u>never</u> get the odor out! Barrels used for apple juice are much easier to clean. Either stand barrels upright and use a pump or siphon to remove the water, or install a spigot in the top and put the barrels on their sides. Attach a food-grade hose and you're in business!

Keep your barrels in a dark, cool place. This helps prevent the growth of green slime. If you fill storage bottles with clean, potable water, such as from your kitchen sink, you don't need to add chlorine (like Clorox), especially if you clean and refill the containers once a year. I don't like the taste of chlorine, and feel that it can be detrimental to my innards, so I prefer to rotate yearly. I will only use chlorine if I feel the water has been contaminated in some way.

Storing water and learning how to purify contaminated water should be among your top priorities in preparing for an emergency. Yes, it takes a bit of planning, a lot of determination, as well as some old fashioned ingenuity. However, it's very important, so don't procrastinate. Dehydration is miserable. It's almost as bad as going two days without washing your hair.

### Project #10 – Happiness is a Hot Meal

**Objective:** To learn how to cook without power and to gather necessary supplies to do so.

**Purchase:**
Purchase a small, fold-up camp stove for use with tuna can fuel
Search out garage sales, estate sales, or auntie's attic for old candles
Invest in a basic Dutch oven. It will be an adventure.

**Action:**
1. Make at least 12 tuna can buddy burners
2. Go to YouTube and watch various videos on Dutch Oven cooking…then attempt it yourself.
3. Decide which cooking methods appeal to you then practice, practice, practice!

## Cooking Without Power

Here's a frustrating scenario: Your town is in the grips of an ice storm and the power is out. Now the kids are asking, "Mom, what's for dinner?"

No power means no oven, no slow cooker, and worst of all, no microwave. Maintaining regular activities after disaster strikes is comforting, especially for children. Serving normal meals will help keep spirits up during this challenging time. So how can you cook a hot meal?

Take a deep breath and remember that a kitchen without power is just like camping out. How do you cook when camping? Over a fire pit? On a Coleman stove? But, you say, I planned for our camping trip. I was prepared. Hello! That's exactly what we're doing here! Planning and preparing!

Let's look at some options. If you have a gas stove, you can cook as normal even without power. Just verify that the gas lines are in working order. A butane stove will utilize normal cookware and can be used indoors with <u>good ventilation,</u> but be aware butane doesn't work well in cold weather. Propane stoves are handy but must only be used outdoors. Another option is foil packs. Almost anything can be tucked into a foil pack and cooked alongside the fire in your wood stove or fireplace.

Sterno, such as used with chafing dishes, works well but in long term storage, it tends to evaporate. For use with chafing dishes or camp stoves, I prefer making tuna can stoves. They are easy to make so I keep ten or twelve in my e-prep kit. Cut cardboard the same height as the can, roll it tightly until the cardboard fills the can. Insert a birthday candle in the center, and then fill the can with melted wax until the cardboard is soaked. Let harden and voila, you have a reliable heat source. The only other item needed is a stand on which to place your pan. These are available at most camping stores or at www.beprepared.com. I bought mine at Wal-Mart for less than $8.00.

I have used both butane and tuna stoves to cook during brief power outages and have sufficient fuel stored for my camp stoves. However, for long term power outages, such as what may occur after an earthquake, I recommend a rocket stove. This efficient stove burns twigs, leaves, and small branches easily gathered in my yard. Its design enables me to use my favorite cast-iron pan or regular kitchen cookware to cook complete meals.

I have three rocket stoves. (It's that plan B and C thing). One is from StoveTec and is my all-time favorite stove. It can be used with charcoal as well as twigs and leaves. They also offer an accessory that enables you to purify water on the stove as well…a very clever device. Naturally, I have one of those as well.

For my 72-hour pack, I have a very lovely rocket stove developed by BioLite. It's…well…simply amazing. It's a tiny stove that fits nicely in my pack, but also has an adapter that enables the heat to be transformed (how, I don't know) into electricity. It will charge anything that can be charged with a USB cable. I think that is simply wonderful. BioLite can be contacted via the Internet at www.biolitestove.com

BioLite is now offering a kettle/pot and a grill attachment as well. They are on my wish list. (Santa, are you listening?)

If you don't want to invest in a cast iron, ceramic, or metal rocket stove, there is one more option. I laughed when I first saw the YouTube video produced by Mitch Ashdown and, of course, just had to try it. I liked it so well, I asked Mitch to allow me to post his video on my website. Either check it out on my website (go to www.emergencypreplady.com and search "video" and it will pop up) or go to YouTube and search wooden wood rocket stove. It's delightful....and it works!

I'm not going to explain it here because seeing it makes it easier to understand...and is so much more enjoyable.

## Sun Ovens

Sun ovens, also known as a solar cookers or solar ovens, are devices which harness the energy of direct sun rays to cook food or to pasteurize water. Most sun ovens are relatively inexpensive since they use no fuel and cost nothing to operate. If you google "how to make a sun oven" you will find that a working oven can easily be made at home from cardboard boxes and some aluminum foil....and a few other items.

### Basic principles of the solar cooker

1. A reflective mirror of polished glass, metal or aluminum foil concentrates the sun's light and heat onto a small cooking area. This makes the energy more concentrated and increasing its heating power.
2. A black surface on the inside of the solar cooker improves the effectiveness by turning the sun's visible light into heat.
3. A tightly sealed glass cover traps the hot air inside the cooker, making it possible to reach cooking temperatures even on cold or windy days.

Sun ovens are a practical preparedness item; however, I strongly suggest you try using one prior to an emergency. Like everything in the preparedness mode, it's best to develop the necessary skills before disaster strikes.

### How to use a solar cooker

Turn the solar cooker towards the sun, set the food inside so that no shadows cover the food, then let sit until the food is cooked. Unlike cooking on the stove top, food in a solar cooker doesn't require constant supervision. Checking the cooker every one or two hours may be required to turn the cooker to face the sun more directly. This is necessary to ensure that shadows from your local environment have not blocked the sunlight.

Cooking time depends on the equipment used, the amount of sunlight at the time, and the quantity of food that needs to be cooked. I have a rather small device and have found I can melt butter in 18 minutes, bake chocolate chip cookies in about 2.5 hours, and rice sufficient for 2 people in 3 hours. Bear in mind that I live in the Pacific Northwest on a plot surrounded by tall fir trees. Cooking times would be extremely different in Arizona.

Sun oven cooking is limited to clear days, especially in the northern regions. Also, we are generally accustomed to eating our main meal of the day in the evening. Unfortunately, that most often is after the sun has set. For these reasons, I don't recommend relying upon a sun oven for your primary cooking device. Always have a plan B…and C, D, and maybe even an E.

At least purchase an insulated storage container so that food cooked in a sun oven can be kept warm until serving time. Hot food will continue cooking for hours if stored in a well-insulated container. Even a basket lined with straw and wrapped in a blanket will work.

Here are a few things I've learned by trial and error. (Okay..lots of error!)

- Don't use aluminum cookware. The shiny surface reflects heat away from the food. Best is black, cast iron cookware or at least black pots.
- Sun ovens require a 10-15% longer cooking time than a regular oven. Plan ahead.
- Food will cook faster when it is in smaller pieces. For example, cut potatoes into bite-sized pieces rather than attempt to bake a whole potato.
- Don't open the solar oven to stir your tasty treat. It's unnecessary, plus opening the solar cooker allows the trapped

heat to escape and therefore slows down the entire cooking process.

- If you wish to make nachos, simply put the cheese over the chips. No lid is needed.
- For a mid-day meal, start in the morning with foods that take longer to cook, then add items such as vegetables, cheese, or soup in the mid-morning.
- Leafy green veggies turn olive drab in a solar cooker. They taste okay, but don't look especially appetizing.
- It is difficult to burn food in a solar cooker.
- Bread and rolls brown on the top rather than on the bottom.
- Food must be started several hours before you plan to eat. Don't wait until you are hungry to start cooking in a sun oven!

**Fireplaces and Campfires**

Cooking over a campfire during a holiday is great fun. Cooking over a campfire during a disaster is a different experience. However, if one plans ahead…which is what emergency preparation is all about…it can supply a family with delicious meals with only a bit more effort that required under normal circumstances.

Most any fireplace can cook as it heats. Even a very small fireplace insert can be pressured to serve as a cooking device when necessary. When my sister and I were children, we looked forward to 'tin foil dinners' as we camped out. These were cubed steaks, thin sliced potatoes, carrots, and onions carefully seasoned and wrapped tightly in foil packages to be tucked into the ashes of our campfire. An indoor fireplace or insert can be utilized for these as well. Sweet corn, potatoes in their skins, fresh caught trout or salmon fillets can also be wrapped in aluminum foil and buried in the ash bank. Just be aware there is no automatic timer to gauge when dinner is ready.

You must have the necessary equipment prior to the emergency! I strongly suggest you invest in a few of the following items:

Long handled skewers. The Roasting Fork is the most basic implement. It's great for hot dogs or marshmallows but other items can be roasted on them as well. They are available in a wide variety of styles. Whichever you chose, I suggest wood handles that don't get hot.

Corn Poppers, Chestnut Roasters, and Meat Grills have metal baskets with long handles. Fill the basket, hold over a bed of coals and in minutes, you'll have a tasty snack. They are also great for cooking kebobs or s'mores. You can even fry hamburgers with these gizmos.

Pie Irons are used for grilling sandwiches, which, as children, my sister and I called "toast-tights." A pie iron has two handles which end in a cast iron, steel, or aluminum plate at the end. The plates are hinged together, which allows a sandwich to be pressed between them.

Bread is buttered on the outside, cheese or other filling fill the interior of the sandwich, then the entire bundle is held over the coals until it is toasted. Yum.

Some versions allow the plates to be used independently for light baking. I highly recommend those made of cast iron. They last forever. Tip: A bit of cooking spray will help keep the food from sticking to the iron.

A few other items I suggest purchasing are these: a sturdy tripod for hanging a pot over a campfire, a basic set of barbeque tools with long handles, a charcoal starter (metal tube for ease of lighting charcoal), several fireproof hot pot holders, and lots and lots of aluminum foil…the heavy duty kind. I also suggest as many Dutch Ovens as you can afford. Treated properly, these will last for many generations.

There are many other tools available for those who really "get into" Dutch oven cooking, but the above are the basics for cooking over a fire.

## Methods

There are three major methods of cooking over a campfire or fireplace: the skewer method, the string method, and the Dutch oven method. Please note: all of these methods require practice. I urge you to try them when it's for "fun" and not during an emergency situation. This way, you can learn from your mistakes when it is still possible to order pizza if the evening meal ends up in the ashes!

### The Skewer Method

Purchase (in advance) a long metal skewer. You may use a long fork sold for roasting marshmallows or fashion a skewer from a coat hanger. It must be sufficient long to hold near the fire without getting so close you burn yourself. Personally, I like the extendable skewers that have wooden handles available at most outdoor stores or Wal-Mart.

Start a fire in your fireplace or outside fire pit. Hardwoods are best, as they get off more heat and make better coals. You want to develop a nice core of hot, glowing embers at the base of the fire.

Choose something to cook that is relatively small. Sausages, hot dogs, and meat balls are good, but it is also possible to cook a small hen or quail. Whatever you cook must be able to be secured on the skewer even as the skewer is rotated. You don't want it to fall off into the ashes.

Place a cookie sheet or roasting pan next to the fire to catch drips. Hold the food over the pan and slowly rotate it so as to 'rotisserie cook' your meal. Don't hold the food too close to the fire. It will quickly burn on the outside and be rare on the inside.

Continue cooking until the meat is golden brown on the outside and completely cooked on the inside. When cooking a small chicken, watch that the juices are clear, not red, and the meat is pulling from the bones. If in doubt, use a meat thermometer to check the internal temperature of your meal.

When cooking is completed, remove the skewer and rest the meat on a plate, covered with foil, to rest for a few minutes before serving.

This method works with either a campfire or an indoor fireplace.

### The String Method

This method is a bit more complicated and requires certain tools. Some directions suggest placing a nail or hook into the wall or mantle above the fireplace. Yikes! I don't recommend that. Rather, I suggest building a small stand. I used a wooden clothes rack from a store that was going out of business as my upright.

Marinate and/or season the roast of your choice. The easiest is a ham with the bone intact. However, it is possible to roast a whole chicken this way. My nephew, who is far cleverer than I, has even rigged up a pork roast with kitchen twine for this purpose.

Tie your roast securely with a very long piece of kitchen twine. You need to truss the roast in such a way that it can be hung by the twine in an upright position.

As before, build a good fire with as much hardwood as possible until you have a good core of embers. To test, hold your hand direct before the front edge of the fireplace opening. If it's uncomfortable, you have good heat!

Hang the roast before the fire from the stand you've created for this purpose. Okay, if you don't mind putting a hole in your wall, you can do that rather than build a stand. The roast should be just in front of the middle of the fire. Make sure the string holding your roast if secure to the nail or stand.

Place a cookie sheet or roasting pan just below the roast to catch the dripping fat and juices.

Now comes the fun part. Give the roast a <u>slight</u> spin so that it rotates on the string. It will spin one direction for a bit and then slowly reverse and begin to rotate the other direction. It should do this for several minutes. If it slows down or stops, simply give it another gentle smack to get it spinning again. Children love to do this.

You may need to add wood to the fire during the cooking process to keep the fire hot. Additionally, you will want to baste your meat periodically. It is also a good idea to wet the string with water to keep it from drying out and possibly breaking. You don't want your lovely roast to fall on the floor!

Use a meat thermometer to determine the interior temperature and continue cooking until it roasted perfectly to your taste. Again, after the roast is done, remove it to a plate, cover with foil and let it rest for a few minutes before carving.

**The Dutch Oven Method**

I briefly mentioned Dutch oven cooking when writing about various fuels, but here is more information about this wonderful cooking method. These ovens were used by early pioneers and are as valuable today as they were in days gone by.

Made of cast iron, a true Dutch oven has three legs, a handle, and a flat lid that allows charcoal briquettes to be stacked on it without falling off. They are available in various sizes. I suggest investing in several, as one can never have too many Dutch ovens!

Dutch oven cooking has developed into an art form and you would do well to visit YouTube to discover some of its methods and challenges. There are even yearly competitions that are delightful to watch. However, for our purpose here, I'm outlining simply the basics.

Prepare your fire as with other methods, using hard woods if possible. Once there are glowing embers at the base of the fire, use fire tongs or a shovel to scoop up some embers and place them to the side of the fire. Prepare the ingredients for your meal and place in the pot and cover, and then carefully place the Dutch oven on top of the hot embers. Place more embers on the top of your Dutch oven to ensure even heating.

You may need to periodically rotate the oven to make sure it heats evenly. Also, it may be necessary to replenish the embers both above and below the oven during a long cooking time.

If possible, store lots of charcoal briquettes strictly for Dutch oven cooking.

I'm not an expert at D.O. cooking, but the following is a "no-fail" recipe for the beginner. This is the traditional Dump Cake made by Boy Scouts everywhere.

**Prep Time:** 10 minutes
**Cook Time:** 40 minutes
**Total Time:** 50 minutes

**Ingredients:**

- 1 29-ounce can sliced peaches
- 1 small can crushed pineapple
- 1 box yellow cake mix
- 2 tablespoons butter
- Vanilla ice cream

**Preparation:**

Dump the peaches and pineapple into a 12-inch Dutch oven and mix. Dump the cake mix evenly on top of the fruit. Spread pats of butter over the top of the cake mix. Using 16 briquettes on top and 12 under the Dutch oven, cook for about 40 minutes or until brown. Be sure to occasionally rotate the Dutch oven and the lid so as to avoid any scorching from possible hot spots. Serve warm with a big scoop of vanilla ice cream.

**Variation:** Use apples and spice cake instead of the ingredients above. Also yummy!

**Servings:**  about 8, unless one guest is my son. Then you must figure on only 4 servings. He loves this recipe!

## All About Fuel

Just in case, let's review the pros and cons of various fuels.

## Coal

It is easy to store coal if you have plenty of room in a dark, dry place away from moving air. Air speeds deterioration and causes the coal to burn much more quickly than desirable.  It can be stored in plastic-lined pits, in bags, boxes or barrels. The key is to keep it dry.

## Wood

Soft woods such as pine, fir or cedar are lightweight and burn very rapidly. This leaves very few coals...and lots of ash. In the Pacific Northwest, most of the commercially sold firewood is fir, which leaves much to be desired.

Hardwoods, such as apple, cherry, oak, or madrona, are slow-burning and make great coals.  Hardwoods are more difficult to start, so I generally recommend using softwood for starting the fire and then adding the hardwood for a longer, slower burning blaze.

Wood for fireplaces and wood stoves is generally sold by the cord. A true cord of wood measures **4ft x 4ft x 8 ft**.  A few years ago, a fellow here in Gig Harbor presumed this little old white-haired lady would make a good mark. He tried to convince me to buy a "cord" of wood from the back of his small pickup…at a full cord price.

Be aware that a true cord will not fit in a small pickup! Even a regular sized pickup requires extended sides to hold a full cord. If necessary, pull out your measuring tape and let all sellers know you understand what constitutes a 'full cord' of firewood.

Also, make sure the wood is well-seasoned. That means that the wood hasn't been recently cut, but has "seasoned" or dried for a least one year. Fresh-cut wood is heavy with moisture and will not burn properly!

## Propane

Propane is an excellent fuel for indoor use, but it does produce carbon dioxide as it burns. This isn't poisonous, but it consumes oxygen. You must always crack a window and make absolutely sure you have sufficient ventilation before using propane indoors.

Propane stores indefinitely and most propane stoves are economical, easy to use, and are certainly convenient. Bear in mind that local laws may limit how much propane you may store both inside and outside your home. Sometimes local permits are required. Check your local requirements before storing a significant amount of propane.

The danger of propane is that it is heavier than air and if the canister leaks, it may pool, creating an explosive atmosphere. In this case, ignition sources such as a water heater or an electrical source can trigger an explosion.

## White gas

This is commonly known as Coleman fuel, since it is the primary fuel used in camping stoves. These stoves are easy to use and are excellent for cooking. However, like charcoal, they produce large amounts of carbon monoxide and should never-ever-ever be used indoors. To do so is risking the lives of yourself and your family.

**Kerosene**

I like kerosene. It is less expensive than other fuels, it is not as explosive as gasoline and Coleman fuel, and it stores well for long periods of time, especially if some fuel additives are added. Store kerosene in plastic containers rather than in metal containers, because the moisture in the kerosene will rust a metal container and you'll have a mess on your hands.

Only use kerosene in kerosene heaters. Not all heaters/stoves are configured to burn kerosene. Also, while kerosene requires very little oxygen compared to charcoal, you still must crack a window to allow sufficient ventilation to avoid asphyxiation.

Always light and extinguish the kerosene stove outside, as at the beginning and ending of the burn, there is a very unpleasant odor. During operation, however, a kerosene stove is fairly odorless.

**Sterno**

Sterno is a jellied petroleum product that is lightweight and easily ignited with a match or even a spark from a flint. One can of Sterno, used judiciously, will cook about five meals. However, as I mentioned before, Sterno will evaporate very easily, so this fuel is not good for long-term storage. I much prefer making the 'buddy burner' with a tuna can and old candle wax.

**Charcoal**

Anyone who has tried Dutch oven cooking is familiar with charcoal. While it must be used outdoors (that's critical), it is the least expensive fuel per BTU that can be safely stored. If stored in air tight containers, it will remain viable for an extended period of time. Do not store charcoal in the paper bag in which it comes, as it will only last a few months before moisture degrades it. Transfer the charcoal to an airtight metal or plastic container and it will keep almost forever.

I keep a stock of five-gallon buckets handy that I purchase for about $2 at either the local bakery or hamburger joint. I replace the lids with

Gamma Seal lids (available at www.beprepared.com) and use these for storing all sorts of things, including my stash of charcoal.

About $65 worth of charcoal will provide all the cooking fuel for a family for about one year. I suggest buying the briquettes at the end of the summer. Ask your retailer for a discount on broken or torn bags.

I strongly suggest you learn about Dutch oven cooking. My nephew, bless him, can cook an entire Thanksgiving dinner…including fresh rolls…in those handy cast iron cookware.

Each briquette will produce about 40 degrees of heat, so one can regulate the heat just as you would an electric oven. Matt firmly states that anything that can be cooked in a slow cooker can be cooked in a Dutch oven over …and under…charcoal, so no special cook books are required.

For tips on how to clean your Dutch oven, or for more ideas on cooking, go to www.lodgemfg.com/videos

**The Bottom Line**

Knowing how to prepare hot meals when you have no electricity is a practical skill to cultivate. It's also important to know how to cook without endangering your family. If you've not thought about survival cooking before, make it a family project to cook without electricity for one weekend. I promise it'll be an adventure!

As with most areas of e-prep, practice makes perfect, so hone your skills before the power goes out! Hopefully, you'll never need these skills but at least you'll know that if the need arises, you will be confident…and prepared!

# Project #11     Let There be Light

**Objective:** Learn various methods of lighting during disasters

**Purchase:** Several rechargeable lanterns, as many flashlights as your budget will allow, and multiple batteries.

**Action:**
1. Make a simple olive oil lamp simply for the experience
2. Search garage sales for candles and jars that might make good lanterns
3. Learn to make wicks from cotton twine.

## Let There Be Light

I don't like to fumble around in the dark. All I need, at my rather advanced age, is to trip over something carelessly left where it shouldn't be ...never, of course, by me... and break a bone. I am also one who tends to go a bit overboard when planning for emergencies.

## Flashlights

My latest 'favorite obsession' is flashlights. I live on a small island where the power goes out when someone sneezes too hard, hence my compulsion to put a flashlight in every nook and cranny of my home and car. When the electricity sputters or a disaster occurs, I'm ready with a handy-dandy flashlight, regardless of my location when the event begins.

Gone are the days when the only choice was a heavy, Army-green monstrosity that required four batteries. Now, flashlights span the gamut from simple, basic lights to sophisticated high-tech gadgets.

There are tiny lights that can hang on a key chain, huge ones that can light up the neighborhood, or ones that strap to a hard hat. There are traditional incandescent bulbs, but also bright, long-lasting LED lights.

One can purchase an ordinary 2D incandescent flashlight for about two dollars. It provides sufficient light for normal use and as long as you stock plenty of replacement bulbs and batteries, there is little need to pay more. For a late-night foray to the refrigerator, these inexpensive lights are more than adequate.

However, for a reliable light for use in an emergency, it's best to spend a bit more. For a flashlight such as you might keep in your car, experts recommend a waterproof, shock-resistant flashlight built for durability. The best LED flashlights are virtually unbreakable, use high-quality LED lights, and can withstand heavy rain or even an unexpected drop in a puddle.

How many flashlights are necessary in the average household? I suggest one in each room, one or more in each car, and one on each key ring. I also have one in my bed bag and one in the garage. I keep at least three in my van...one in each door panel and one on a lanyard in my 72-hour pack.

Don't forget batteries. I buy regular AA and D batteries in bulk, since I use them in both flashlights and my portable radio. I also buy a few rechargeable batteries. If you buy rechargeable batteries, you must also purchase a charger. Buy two: one electric that plugs into your home outlet, and one solar powered for long-term power outages. Be aware that rechargeable batteries must be emptied then recharged within a short period of time to remain effective. For this reason, rechargeable batteries are not good for 'buying, sticking away and forgetting."

Now that batteries are available which are guaranteed effective for up to ten years, I tend to ignore rechargeable batteries.

There are also flashlights that can be charged by solar power, by hand cranking, or by shaking. My personal favorite is the Wavelength. It is an AM/FM radio, a cell phone charger and rechargeable flashlight all in one. A hand crank charges the battery which will produce about thirty minutes light from one minute of cranking.

Check your flashlights and batteries about every six months and change them if necessary. Dead batteries or broken bulbs will leave you stumbling around in the dark.


### Lanterns

Ah, the blessings of modern technology! We now have available a wide variety of lanterns to supply light during a power outage.  However, remember that alternative sources of light must be purchased prior to an event when they are reasonably inexpensive and readily available. During an event, it is often very difficult…or impossible…to obtain even the rudimentary device.

Most localized power outages are caused by hurricanes or winter storms. If an event is of a short-term, battery operated lanterns will most likely suffice. However, the prudent may wish to stock up on batteries, as batteries do die eventually.

I have three lanterns. One is an electric model that stays plugged into the house circuit. It will light for about 20 hours straight without recharging and is my "Plan A." My "Plan B" is a battery operated lantern for which I also have stored multiple extra batteries.  Now that Energizer has batteries guaranteed for up to 10 years in storage, I have indulged my passion for extra batteries.

The third lantern, my "Plan C" is Goal Zero Lighthouse 250 Lumen Rechargeable lantern I found at Emergency Essentials. It can provide 45 hours of light and can be recharged from the sun, a USB port, or via hand crank.  Remember I spoke of the BioLite Rocket stove that burns twigs and leaves and can charge anything that can be charged with a USB port?  Well….voila! Now I have a lantern that can be easily recharged…forever. It was rather expensive, but it is worth its price in peace of mind!

There are several solar-powered lanterns that can offer light even after cloudy days. Those solar walkway lamps that line outdoor paths can be brought in at night to provide some light.

Kerosene lanterns and gas lanterns are available at most camping outfitters. You must be sure to have sufficient fuel stored safely away from the house for these. I don't like gas lanterns as they are very noisy. Also, I'm not one to store large amounts of volatile fuel near my home. There are 30 acres of timber behind my house and the last thing I need in an emergency is a forest fire!

A kerosene lantern with a 1" wick will burn approximately 45 hours per quart of kerosene. They will also burn a scented lamp oil which can replace kerosene…and smell better. This lamp oil is generally available at hardware stores such as Ace Hardware or Home Depot.

Kerosene lanterns are much dimmer than a two-mantle Coleman lantern.

## Candles

Candles do supply light, but there are drawbacks to using candles as your main source of light. First, common decorative candles have a short life. Emergency candles…those graceless stubbies… can have up to 100 hours of burn time and an indefinite shelf life.

Tallow candles burn bright and longer and are fairly smoke-free compared to wax candles. They must be stored in a cool, dry place. Try storing your candles in the freezer. It will make them burn longer and without dripping.

I recommend storing a minimum of 360 candles…one per day and more if possible. One simply cannot have too many candles. Additionally, make sure you have multiple broad-based candle holders. Candles are extremely dangerous indoors due to high fire danger, especially if you have children. For this reason, be sure to have a good quality fire extinguisher in each room where candles are used.

I love estate sales, mostly because I can purchase partially burned candles for pennies. The wax can then be used to make tuna can "buddy" burners, can be used as is, or can be recycled into new candles.

It's easy to make new wicks from kitchen twine (see tips for directions). Never throw candle ends away. Recycle them for emergencies!

**Odds and ends about candles**

- White or cream candles will burn brighter than dark ones.
- To increase the light, place an aluminum foil reflector behind each candle or place them before a mirror.
- Votive candles will burn for approximately 15 hours when placed in an empty jelly jar.
- A glass dish, a wick and a bottle of salad oil will provide hundreds of hours of candle light.
- A candle in a can may be purchased with several wicks for a brighter light.
- A can of Crisco can double as an emergency candle. (See tips for directions)
- Fifty and One Hundred hour candles are available in both solid and liquid form.
- Trench candles can be made from a narrow strip of cloth, newspapers, and salvaged candle wax. (See tips for directions.)
- Keep children and pets away from candles. Scented candles often smell good enough to eat, but are not suitable as food!
- The most important tip for burning votive candles is to burn them in a tight-fitting container. They will last longer.
- Candles smoke if the wick is too long, no matter what type of wax is used. Trim wicks often.
- Scented candles will smoke more than unscented ones.
- That "mushroom" on the wick forms when the wick needs to be trimmed.
- An easy way to trim wicks is to use nail clippers.
- Never lean too close over a burning candle, especially if you use hair spray! It can ignite.
- Never leave a burning candle unattended. This is how accidental fires start. Let me repeat that. NEVER leave a burning candle unattended.

- In desperate times, remember than a crayon will burn for several minutes even without a wick. A good brand of crayon must be used, such as Crayola.

## Oil Lamps

Oil lamps have been around since…well, forever. In ancient times, these handy lamps were to only method of light otherwise dark areas.

An olive oil lamp is safe, easy to use, and far less expensive than some other options.

Bear in mind that you don't need to use the expensive culinary 'extra virgin' olive oil. For lamps, buy the least expensive olive oil you can find.

In many areas of the globe, lampante oil is used. This is the most chemically refined olive oil which has no nutritional value and generally is not acceptable for consumption. Unfortunately, this type of olive oil is rarely found in America.

Other types of cooking oils can be used in an oil lamp, but many smoke profusely or give off a funny, stale odor. Olive oil burns clean, bright, and will last many hours on a single wick.

Vegetable oil lamps have a number of advantages over candles and mineral oil lamps. First, they are very cheap to run since they can burn even used cooking oils. The fumes are less toxic than those of paraffin candles or mineral oil lamps. Additionally, vegetable oil is easier to store in bulk.

It is easy to make an oil lamp. The basic elements are a piece of twisted wire, a length of cotton twine, some vegetable oil and a jar in which to hold it all. If you don't feel especially creative, the individual elements or completed lamps can be purchased at many hardware stores or at Lehman's. Lehman's also offers a booklet called, "I Didn't Know that Olive Oil Would Burn" that is quite informative.

Wicks can be purchased, but they are easy to make as well. When the prepping bug strikes, one symptom is that one is always trying to see what secondary use can be made of items normally to be discarded. I recently discovered that an old cotton shoe lace makes a great wick!

Never discard rancid olive oil. Rather, set it aside for use in your oil lamp. If you don't have olive oil, other types of oils can be used; even grease can be used in a pinch. However, some oils other than olive oil will smoke and grease will make your home smell like someone burned the popcorn.

To make a lamp, gather the following materials:
1. A wide-mouth glass jar – a quart size canning jar is perfect
2. A short length of flexible steel wire about 2-2.5 times the height of the jar.
3. a long nail
4. A wick – new or recycled cotton twine
5. Olive oil

Wrap one end of the wire around the nail several times to create a wick stand about 2 inches tall. This will be the part that will hold the wick. Pinch the top onto about 2 inches of the wick so that about a quarter inch of the wick will stick up above the wire coil. The other end of the wick will be soaking in the olive oil.

Form the other end of the wire into a long hook that is about the same height as the jar. This will both hold the wire in the jar and doubles as a handle to pull up the wick for lighting.

Add sufficient olive oil to the jar until the level is just under where the wick is pinched by the wire.

Don't allow the wick to stick up above the wire coil more than 2 inches. If so, it will smoke.

The olive oil will be drawn up the wick where it vaporizes and is burned by the flame. It only takes a few ounces of oil to burn your lamp for several hours.

Lamp oil tends to be less expensive than olive oil, but I like the 'double duty' of olive oil.

The benefits of olive oil lamps are that they are reliable, burn brightly, and if the lamp gets knocked over, it stops burning. Therefore, an olive oil lamp is far safer than candles!

If you wish to make your own wicks, follow the following directions:

Purchase 100% cotton twine, put several lengths into a bowl with a little water and cover with good old-fashioned table salt. Squeeze to remove excess water, then hang overnight until it is completely dry. For a wider wick for larger lamps, either buy flat wicks or cut a 100% cotton tea towel into 1 inch stripes, soak in salt, then dry. This may not result in as efficient as wick as a commercially made wick, but in a pinch, it will work.

# Project #13   First Aid Kits

**Objective:**  To gather basic first aid supplies for the various kits

**Action:**
1.  Sign up for a first aid class with your local Red Cross or through your local Emergency Management Service department. You may also find online disaster skills training courses that can be done in your robe and bunny slippers from the convenience of your own home.
2.  Don't discard that old bed sheet. Tear it into strips for use as bandages

First Aid - Beyond Band-Aids

"OUCH! Mom, I need a band-aid!" This was a common cry when my son was young. He was a skateboarder, a rock climber, surfer, and a get-into-mischief professional. Due to his heart-stopping escapades, I kept a well-stocked first aid kit with plenty of band-aids and Neosporin.

His father kept his doctor's bag handy as well, which contained, among other items, suturing materials. More than once I found him at the kitchen table, calmly stitching Brian back together. This was in normal times... nothing more serious than jumping off the roof into the pool and hitting the edge. Can you imagine what supplies might be needed in a real disaster?

What constitutes a major disaster? Like beauty, that's in the eye of the beholder. It can be regional ...like an earthquake...or individual...like having chain saw issues while perched on a ladder. Yep. My son did that too.

A well-stocked first aid kit, kept within easy reach, is a necessity for every home. In a major disaster, a few band-aids and some Neosporin will not suffice. Someone you love may be cut, burned, scraped, smashed or broken. If you have supplies, you are better prepared to help ease their pain, stop bleeding, stabilize broken bones and prevent infection. Or save a life!

Emergency preparedness is realizing that something serious could happen, then preparing for that event. A major step in planning for your family's safety and comfort is to gather essential supplies in advance. You can't say, "Hold on, sweetie. I'll run to the store and buy some stuff. Please don't bleed all over the carpet while I'm gone!"

Supplies gathered ahead of time will help you handle an emergency at a moment's notice. Generally, a moment is all the advanced warning you're going to get.

Ready-made first aid kits are available but most are created for 'normal' situations. I suggest adding additional items for those times when there might be more serious injuries but medical help is unavailable for several days...such as what might happen if an earthquake were to hit your home town. Under the section labeled "Lists" is a comprehensive listing of emergency supplies you may wish to include in your first aid kit.

But, a word of warning here. Having the supplies is one thing; knowing what to do with those supplies is another! Being trained to treat injuries can make a big difference in an emergency situation.

For example, during that January shooting rampage in Tucson where the senator was shot, I was amazed at the number of average citizens who, when suddenly confronted with a horrific event, were prepared to assist gravely wounded victims. At the Safeway store that day, lives were saved by ordinary people who had the foresight to take basic first aid training. They were prepared for the unthinkable.

Take a first aid course and do it now. A little research in your local area will turn up groups who offer first aid courses for a small fee. Check www.heartstartsafety.com or your local Red Cross. There are, I believe, even courses offered online.

Don't leave anything to chance. Rather, be prepared when someone you love says, "Ouch!"

Now, normally, I suggest a family have three first aid kits.

The first, and smallest, is a basic first aid kit containing bandages, antibiotic ointment, burn medication, sterile gauze, tweezers, aspirin, sterile eye wash, and cold tablets suitable for adults and children. This is the kit suitable to keep under the seat of the car.

The intermediate kit could fit in a fairly good-sized tackle box and is suitable to keep either in the house or in the family car. It should be a well-maintained first aid kit with some emergency medical supplies.

The last is a well-stocked medical kit, capable of handling anything from the onset of a cold to a severe laceration. It is your home pharmacy for dire circumstances and contains a wide variety of medical supplies and medications. I think of it as what I would want if cut off from medical services for an extended period of time.

There are a few items that one simply must include in all first aid kits.

- Dressings: these are small or large squares of non-adhesive, absorbent dressings. They serve to cover protect a wound as well as to stop bleeding.
- Roller bandages: these are elasticized roller bandages, necessary to know dressings in place, apply pressure to bleeding wounds, to assist in splinting fractures and to stabilize joint sprains. Stock a variety of sizes.
- Triangular bandages: These can be used for making slings, splinting fractures or stabilizing sprains.
- Band-aids: Useful for protecting minor wounds, purchase lots of them in various sizes.
- Tape: One can never have too much tape. I prefer "Elastoplast" tape as it always sticks well.
- Gloves: These are for your protection as well as the one you are treating. Always assume anyone you are treating has a blood borne disease. (Not so important when dealing with family members). Secondly, you wish to reduce the chance of infection when dealing with wounds. Nitrile gloves are more expensive than latex, but many people are allergic to latex.

Each home should have a basic medical supply kit that is individualized to the family's needs. Most people have band-aids and antibiotic ointment, but everyone should have some additional items as well, especially those that can stop dehydration, bleeding, or diarrhea. There are circumstances where emergency responders cannot reach injured or ill victims in a reasonable period of time. It is for these times that we prepare. Having necessary medical supplies in your home could possibly save someone's life!

Remember, medicines can break down and spoil, especially if exposed to moisture, temperature fluctuations, and light. Aspirin, for example, will break down most easily when exposed to a tiny bit of moisture. Therefore, the bathroom is the worst place to keep medications…yet that's exactly where most of us keep them.

Select an area of your home that is cool, dark, and out of children's reach. Check expiration dates periodically to ensure the medications are still viable.

# Project #14   Sanitation – a dirty, unpleasant subject

**Objective:** To understand the basic nature of sanitation, why it is important to maintain good sanitation during a disaster, and to gather needed supplies.

**Purchase:** Lime (non-garden variety), multiple sturdy garbage bags, buckets or portable potty, lots of toilet paper, handy wipes, and disinfectants.

**Action:** Create a sanitation kit as an essential step in keeping your family healthy.

**Keeping Clean**

What if…? Can you imagine what it would be like if your trash wasn't picked up each week? What would it smell like if left for several weeks? What if inside the trash were dirty diapers, rotting meat and food, and perhaps even human waste? E.coli and bacteria would invade everything and the potential for disease and epidemics would be overwhelming.

Following a major disaster, sanitation facilities may not be available. Water and sewer lines may have been broken, leaving little option for disposal of waste. Unfortunately, generally more people die in the aftermath of a major disaster due to poor sanitation than during the event itself.

Cleanliness is essential to good health. A sanitation kit is a critical component of any emergency preparedness plan.

First, clean water is a precious commodity during a disaster and must be reserved for drinking and cooking only. For cleansing bodies, consider alternatives to water such as rubbing alcohol, towelettes, shaving lotions, and face creams and hand lotions. These, of course, must be stored prior to an emergency.

A wet wash cloth can serve to wash faces; a spray bottle can double as a shower when necessary. Some camp stores sell a 'sun shower' …a plastic bag that can be filled with water, heated by the sun, and used for a shower. Mine holds about two gallons of water…not enough for a long, hot shower, but sufficient to get the top layer of grime off and to rinse my hair.

Consuming contaminated water and food can cause diarrhea, food poisoning and other nasty diseases. Take steps to protect against these diseases by keeping body and hands clean, as well as making sure dishes and pots used for cooking are clean and disinfected as well. The best disinfectant is a solution of one part liquid chlorine bleach to ten parts water. Dry bleach is caustic and not safe to use for this purpose

An easy way to avoid having to wash dishes is to use paper plates. Every emergency stash should include several stacks of paper plates and cups.

As much as possible, continue your basic hygiene routine, such as brushing your teeth, washing your face, combing your hair, and at least rudimentary bathing. This will help prevent the spread of disease as well as maintain at least a semblance of normalcy.

Keep your fingers out of your mouth and your hands away from your face. It's said that during normal circumstances, one touches their face at least 3-5 times per minute. Do the math! That's a lot of times to risk spreading an infection.

Keep your clothing as clean and dry as possible, especially your underwear and socks.

Unfortunately, after a disaster, we could be facing weeks of sanitary problems which can bring serious health risks. There is always a risk of disease from eating or drinking anything contaminated with flood water or refuse from a neighbor's yard. Many of these diseases are spread by uncontrolled or improperly handled sewage. So…how do we deal with this subject?

### Emergency Toilet Flushing 101

In planning for emergencies, one phrase dominates my thinking…"What if…? What if Gig Harbor experiences severe flooding? An earthquake? What if…?

Recently, I watched three TV commercials for Angel Soft toilet paper. They were entitled, "Uncomfortable Bathroom Moments" and they were quite hysterical.

I giggled, but then wondered, "Ohmigosh! What if people couldn't flush the toilet? What if an earthquake or other catastrophe caused damage to the water lines?"

Most toilets require water in order to flush and therefore cannot be used when water service is interrupted. What little water may remain in the lines isn't generally sufficient to flush the wastes down the sewer. Attempting to flush simply results in clogging the system, which will then back up, making your living situation much more unpleasant.

Even if limited water is available, local authorities may prohibit flushing toilets, sinks, and other fixtures connected with soil pipes. If the sewer mains are broken and backups occur…well, you get the not-so-pretty picture.

Families should know emergency methods of waste disposal and have the necessary supplies on hand. The lack of sanitation facilities following a major disaster and the failure to properly dispose of human wastes can lead to very serious problems such as typhoid, diarrhea, and dysentery. It is also important to dispose of sewage in ways that will avoid contamination of water supplies used for drinking, cooking, and bathing.

The flush toilet can be converted to non-flush with the use of plastic bags, which would be considerably less uncomfortable than sitting on a bucket. First, don rubber gloves. Turn off the water supply to the toilet and remove all the water in the bowl. Line the empty toilet bowl with a heavy-duty plastic bag.

After use, add a small amount of deodorant or disinfectant such as Pine Sol, tie the bag securely and deposit it (no pun intended) in a large garbage can with a tight fitting lid that has also been lined with a sturdy trash bag. Hopefully, the city will eventually advise where to dispose of these bags.

My friend Vicki had to do this once. At that time, she was short on thick garbage bags so had to resort to using the heaviest retail bags she could find in her cabinet. "Grocery bags were too thin so I had to use Nordstrom bags for poopie," she complained later, "That's just not right!" Fortunately, the situation was resolved quickly.

If you use a gravity-fed septic system, check all pipes prior to flushing your toilet. If all is well, you may flush your toilet with non-potable water such as rainwater collected from the roof or recycle water used for washing dishes, clothes, or bodies.

### Building a makeshift toilet

If your toilet bowl is unusable and you find you must use a bucket, make a toilet seat from two boards placed parallel to each other across the bucket. It's not great, but it is better than trying to sit on the rim of the bucket!

Toilet-flushing probably isn't the most fascinating topic you'd wish to discuss on a lovely afternoon, but it's important to plan for all basic needs in case an emergency situation occurs.

### The Bottom Line (again, no pun intended)

If you are using your regular toilet lined with garbage bags, add a small amount of disinfectant to the bag, tie it securely and dispose of it in a large trash can with a tight fitting lid which has also been lined with a sturdy trash bag. Dispose of these bags as directed by city or county officials.

If sanitary services are not quickly restored, it may be necessary to bury garbage and human wastes in the ground to avoid the spread of disease by rats, mice, and other critters.

If this becomes necessary, dig a pit two to three feet deep and at least fifty feet from any water supply. Some areas may prohibit the burying of human waste, so listen to the radio for instructions.

Be prepared for an unpleasant situation by purchasing a box of heavy-duty garbage bags with ties, a medium-size plastic bucket with a tight lid, a couple of bottles of household chlorine bleach, a small shovel (for digging), several bottles of liquid soap or detergent, and lots of toilet paper. If there are babies in your family, you will also want to stock up on disposable and non-disposable diapers and assorted wipes. Don't forget assorted women's needs as well.

Go ahead and splurge a bit. Buy a spare toilet seat, a couple of bottles of pine-scented disinfectant and perhaps a few aromatic candles…just in case!

## Project #16   Precious Pets

**Objective:** Create a plan for caring for your pets during a disaster

**Action:** Gather documentation records for your pets: IDs, immunization records, and a list of any medications they take.

### Emergency Preparedness for Pets

If you are like most pet owners, your animals are valued members of your family. Many of you would risk life and limb to save your precious pets during a disaster. However, the likelihood that you and your animals will survive an emergency such as a fire, flood, or earthquake depends largely on emergency planning done today.

Each of you, as individuals, should take personal responsibility for the safety and well being of your family…and that includes your pets. Don't rely on FEMA, the Red Cross, or your church to provide supplies and assistance. While these groups may be available to offer some help, they probably won't be able to care for animals.

What should you do to ensure your pet's survival? Plan, prepare, purchase and practice. You must plan where Fido or Fluffy will stay, prepare a way to safely evacuate them, and purchase the necessary supplies to meet their needs throughout the disaster. Then practice so your plan becomes instinctive...even when you are under stress.

Here are some ideas to consider when creating an emergency plan for your pets.

- Microchip your pets. This is one of the best ways to ensure you and your pets are reunited if you become separated. Keep the microchip registration up-to-date and make sure to include at least one out-of-area phone number. Out-of-state numbers may be more easily reached in a disaster than local numbers.

- Take photos of your pet with your cell phone. If you get separated, the photos may help locate your missing pet.

- Keep a collar and tag with current phone numbers listed on your pets, even if they are indoor-only animals. If your home is damaged during a disaster, they could easily escape and become frightened, confused and lost.

- If you must leave your home, take your pets with you if at all possible. Remember, animals generally will not be allowed inside public shelters due to health, safety or other concerns. (Service animals are an exception.) Plan a separate shelter for your pets.

- Prepare a way to confine or control your pet during evacuation. This may be more difficult if you are not able to evacuate in your own vehicle, so again, plan ahead. A leash, muzzle, or cage may be needed.

- Assemble an emergency supply kit which includes pet food, water, medications, medical records, leashes, ID tags and other appropriate supplies. Put this kit near those you have prepared (hopefully) for the human members of your family so it will be readily available.

There is a wealth of information available regarding pet safety during stressful times. The Red Cross offers a Pet First Aid booklet, and more ideas can be found at www.ready.gov or at www.petfinder.com/disaster

A disaster can occur at anytime and in any place. It may be a personal catastrophe, an event that troubles only Gig Harbor, or a disaster that affects the entire Pacific Northwest. Whatever happens, planning ahead is the key to keeping your pets safe when disaster strikes.

# Project #16   Communications

**Objective:**  Obtain ways to communicate with family members as well as to gain information from local and national sources during an emergency

In the musical "Flower Drum Song" there is a song that complains about the 'other generation' and asks "How will we ever communicate without communication?"

This is a fair question for the beginning prepper to ask as well. One thing most all natural disasters have in common is that there is an almost total loss of the ability to communicate with the outside world.

Once power is lost, telephone services stop. Cell phone service is either non-existent or is so terribly overwhelmed that no one can get through. Text message have a better chance of getting through the gridlock, but even these are not guaranteed to be successful. Frankly, it is scary how vulnerable our communication systems are and how dependent we are on them.

During a disaster, when normal communication is limited or non-existent, having an alternate communication device on hand will be extremely helpful.  For example, a wind-up or battery operated radio will let one know if the disaster is of national or local proportions as well as what to expect.  If weather is the problem, a NOAA weather station may give advice as to what steps to take to protect your loved ones. The amateur radio system may be able to relay messages to distant friends and relatives as to your safety, thus relieving anxieties. Even walkie-talkies can be helpful in some situations, such as an earthquake.

There are a few items that should be included in your preparations. Secure a flashing emergency light, beacon, or signal flares. Most camping stores will offer these items or they can be found at www.beprepared.com. Purchase a compass for all members of your family, even the little ones, and teach them to use it. A two-way radio is desirable, and a battery operated or wind-up hand radio, preferably a NOAA weather radio, is a necessity.

If you wish to "go for the gold" and set up a more involved emergency communication system, consider these factors: it should be easy to operate, have an effective range, have protection against interference, be relatively inexpensive, be readily available and be able to operate off-the-grid.

## Conclusion

Well, if you've read this far, the prepping bug must have hit you! Hopefully, you will want to do it and do it right now! That's a good thing, but give reasonable care and thought to the process. Don't buy gear just to have cool gear. It must be useful…and you must know how to use it! Don't buy foodstuffs that you will never eat. Rather, take your time and make wise decisions.

So now that you've read the entire manual, get off your bum and get started! Plan, purchase and prepare for a period of time lasting from three days to three weeks. When you've completed that process, you'll feel great!

But, don't leave it at that. Many disasters that we possibly will face in the near future will last longer than 3 weeks. That will be the subject of the next manual in this series: Three weeks to three months.

## Clever Ideas

**Trench Candles** can be used for lighting or for fuel in your fireplace.
1.  Lay a narrow strip of cloth or twisted string on the edge of a stack of 8-10 newspapers. This will serve as a wick.
2.  Roll the papers as tightly as possible, leaving about ¾ inch of the wick extending at <u>cach</u> end. (You're going to make two trench candles)
3.  Tie the roll firmly with string or wire at 3 inch intervals.
4.  With a small saw, cut about 1 inch above each tie and pull the cut sections into cone shapes. Make sure to pull the center string in each piece to the top of the cone to serve as a wick.
5.  Melt paraffin in a double boiler (or in a can set in a pan of boiling water) Soak the pieces of paper candles in the paraffin for about two to three minutes. Make sure the candles are well saturated with the paraffin.
6.  Remove the candles and allow to dry thoroughly.

**Fire Starters:**
-   Cotton swabs dipped in recycled candle wax become instant fire starters. They are lightweight, inexpensive (get the swabs at your local Dollar store) and take up very little room.
-   Roll cotton balls in petroleum jelly, let sit in the sun for a few minutes until all the ball is well-coated, and then store in recycled pill containers.
-   Recycle a cardboard egg carton by filling it with 'match light' charcoal. Fill each eggcup with one briquette. Do not use Styrofoam egg cartons…they will not work! Light the carton and the fire will spread, lighting the charcoal as well. Easy…and dust free!

**Inexpensive Lamp:**
    Attach a headlamp with the light directly against a cleaned milk jug. Fill the jug with water and you have an instant lantern with soft, ambient light.

**Bug-away:**

- Mix one part tea tree oil with 2 parts water and put the mixture into a spray bottle. It will keep ticks away.
- Add bundles of sage to your campfire to keep mosquitoes away.

**Bed Sheet Bandages:**

During a major disaster, commercial bandages may be in short supply, so rolled bandages, or what used to be called "missionary bandages" are often needed. This is a great use for old bed sheets, preferably those that are white and made of cotton or a cotton blend. Here are the instructions:

1. Pre-wash the sheets.
2. Rip into strips two to four inches wide. The easiest way to do this is to snip the hems, selvages and if using a fitted sheet, remove the elastic. Fold the sheet in half so that you have the longest strips possible. Snip the folded sheet every 3 inches then tear the sheet into strips.
3. Bandages can be made from just one strip the length of a standard bed sheet or can be sewn together end to end for a longer, continuous roll.
4. Assemble strips into rolls about one to two inches in diameter.
5. Roll tightly and evenly and pull off loose threads.
6. Secure with masking tape to keep the bandages from unrolling. Do not use pins, strings, or rubber bands to hold the rolls together. Masking tape works best.

Rather than discard an old bed sheet, use it to make some roller bandages. They store easily and just might come in handy if… or when… disaster strikes.

**Crisco Candles**

Here's a weird fact for you. Crisco was originally a candle company. Now, a large can of Crisco can make a very useful emergency candle. True, I would chose other candles for use first, but sometimes fate steps in and a can of Crisco may be all you have available.. so this is good information to know.

Any size tub of Crisco will do, but the standard 48 oz. tub will last longer. You will need a 10 inch wick… either homemade or commercially purchased. Open the tub then using a stick (I used a chopstick) make a hole in the center of the Crisco. Make sure you go all the way to the bottom of the tub.

Place your wick on the top of the hole. A pre-made wick will have the little piece of metal on the end. If you are using a homemade wick, use either a recycled metal piece from an old candle or shape a paper clip into a round circle and fasten the wick to it. Having a piece of metal on the end of the wick makes it easier to push through the Crisco to the bottom of the tub.

Hold the wick in one hand and use the other to push the wick down the hole. If you keep the wick straight and taut, you should be able to get the wick to the bottom without much trouble. Make sure you work it all the way down to the bottom.

Don't worry if the hole seems big. It will fill in naturally as you burn the candle. Just smooth the top area around the hole with your finger so as to lock the wick in place.

Light the wick and allow it to burn the top part off. This will only take a few seconds. Once the fire hits the Crisco, it will start burning like a regular candle.

That's all there is to it. The candle will burn for a long time, but as it burns down, will give less and less light. I've often wondered what kind of container I could put the Crisco in that would be translucent but so far, haven't found anything. If you come up with something, please let me know!

**Newspaper Logs**

You can make fuel for your fireplace by using newspapers. They are easy to make and create an inexpensive source of heat. However, be prepared to get your hands dirty. Don't worry... it is fun!

First, eliminate any colored print. You don't want to burn the chemicals used to make the colors.

To get a solid log, you must first change the structure of the newspaper to that of paper mache. In other words, you must change the paper to pulp. This can be done with a rubber mallet.

You will need lots of newspapers, a strong 5 gallon bucket, a rubber mallet and a dowel about one inch thick. It's best to work on a concrete surface… you'll see why in a minute.

Fold the newspapers and put three or four into the bucket and cover with water. They may float to the top so be prepared to push them down with a stick. I suggest soaking the newspapers for a couple of days, but one day will suffice if need be. To speed up the softening process, put a squirt or two of detergent in the water. You may also add a wee bit of flour to the water which will help the paper bind together.

Now comes the fun part. Take the wet, soggy newspapers out of the bucket, drain some of the water off, and then lay it out on the hard surface. Don't do this on your kitchen floor!

Starting at the top of the newspaper, hit it with the mallet and work your way down until you reach the bottom. Then, carefully lift the mashed newspaper and flip it over. Now hit the other side with the mallet.

Next, take the dowel and place it at the narrow side of the newspaper. Your dowel should be slightly longer than the width of the newsprint. Curl the paper around it and start to roll. As you roll, squeeze so that everything is well compressed. When you finish, you'll need to be sure you have pressed the end of the newspaper into the log so it doesn't unravel.

When you are finished, squeeze and shape the log with your hands to get it as solid as possible. Next, turn it up on its end and slide the log off the dowel. Use your thumbs to press in the ends of the log to create a neat, compact log. Remember to do both ends.

Here is where you may wish to wash your hands! (Giggle, giggle, snort, giggle)

Put the logs in the sun to dry. It is best to make the logs during the summer, as without a strong sunny day, it will take weeks for the logs to dry. In Washington State, it took my logs three weeks to dry even though it was fairly sunny. In Phoenix, it would require a shorter time period. They will also dry faster if placed on a drying rack. I once used an old screen door for this.

Make a lot of these during the summer when the weather is conducive for this project. In the winter, you'll be glad you did!

Warning: Kiddies will want to assist you, but I've found their enthusiasm wanes quickly.

# Lists:

### Tools

Good quality tools can last a lifetime if properly cared for. Remember, a person is only as good as their tools.

- 32-gallon garbage can with a tight fitting lid
- Flashlight with alkaline batteries, at least one hand-crank flashlight for each member of the household, extra flashlights for each vehicle, and multiple extra batteries. Try to purchase flashlights and other electronics that use the same size batteries.
- Heavy rope
- Duct tape. Lots and lots of duct tape
- Bic lighters and matches. Store in waterproof containers. Be sure to buy 'light anywhere' matches rather than those that require the box to light.
- Good, sturdy multi-tool
- If you have pets, purchase a leash, pet carrier and an extra set of ID tags.

### Bed Bags

When putting together your bed bags, think what items you would desperately need in the first 10 minutes if suddenly forced from your home. I've listed items for cold weather, simply because one can always discard extra clothing, but if you're cold, you're <u>cold</u>! Each bag should be individualized, but at a minimum, should include the following:

- Cold weather clothing including shirt, pants, jacket, waterproof poncho, hat, gloves, socks, boots.
- Dust mask
- Eye protection

- Tube tent
- Tarp (at least one per family)
- Water (at least one bottle)
- Snack (high energy bars are good)
- Whistle
- Flashlight and extra batteries
- Knife
- Personal care kit (toothbrush, paste, lotion, required meds, etc)
- Several emergency blankets (Mylar type)
- Small roll of duct tape
- Small length of rope
- Fire materials: matches, kindling, or other fire starter
- Several heat packs

Additionally, make sure to pin to the inside of your bag extra keys to the car, house, and/or storage shed.

### 72 hour packs

This is my ideal 72-hour pack, but it is pretty heavy. You may wish to 'lighten the load' depending upon your particular situation. You may also be able to spread some of these items over several back packs…for example, not each member need carry a tent. One per family may suffice. I'm a single little old lady, so must have all my needs in one pack. Keep my 72- hour back pack in my car, but I also have a little fold-up wheeled dolly I can use if necessary.

### Shelter

- Storm shelter or tube tent
- Poncho/survival suit
- Hat – gloves – bandana
- Umbrella
- Plastic 5x7 tarp
- Garbage bags (big, black ones)
- Sleeping bag or blankets

**Light – Warmth**
- Flashlight & batteries
- Lantern & batteries
- Candles – waterproof matches
- 100 hr candle
- Emergency reflective blanket
- Heat pack  (4)
- Light sticks (4)
- Set of sweats (top and pants, tee shirt
- Under garments
- Boots/socks
- Fire starting kit such as cotton balls dipped in Vaseline and flint

**Food - Water– Preparation**
- Folding stove & heat source
- Cook set
- Can opener
- Utensils – cup
- 72 hour food pack*  (see below)
- Purifying water bottle
- Water purification tablets
- Aluminum foil
- Hot pad holders
- Stainless steel cooking pot
- Small fry pan

**First Aid – Personal items**
- Small first aid kit
- Toothbrush, paste, and soap
- Handy wipes – tissues
- Lip balm - hand lotion

- Hand sanitizer
- Safety pins
- Wash cloth
- Sunscreen
- Insect repellent
- Toilet paper
- Small hand towel
- Bottle of potassium iodide tablets
- Purse pack with Medications

## Tools

- Shovel or trowel
- Pocket knife
- Fixed blade knife
- Whistle
- Pliers
- 2 screwdrivers
- Flares
- Hammer
- Hatchet
- Saw/finger saw
- Crowbar
- Tent stakes
- Assorted nails
- Duct tape
- Dust mask
- Plastic bags
- Rope or cord 50`
- Bungee cord
- Clothes pins

## Communication

- Radio with batteries
- Emergency addresses
- Pen, pencil, notepad
- Spare glasses
- Flash drive with important papers
- Money- $20 in small bills plus $20 in quarters/dimes/nickels
- Alternate IDs for each family member, preferably with photos

## 72 Hour Food Bucket

This is my list which I've included as a sample. Create your own individualized list determined by your family's food preferences.

- 3 cans tuna
- 3 cups ready-to-eat soup
- 3 cans soup  (no pop tops!)
- 3 boxes raisins
- 3 candy bars
- 12 breakfast bars
- 12 packages cider mix
- 3 rolls crackers
- 3 large bottles water
- 3 Thrive freeze dried dinners – just add water
- 1 large bag lemon drops
- Assorted freeze dried fruits

## First Aid supplies

The following is the list I've created for my own use. You may find some items are unnecessary for your family or think of others that may be required. This list is a starting point...not an end-all.

- Band aids (lots)
- Roller bandages
- Sterile gauze

- Triangular bandages (can be used as a sling)
- Antiseptic solution such as betadine
- Antibiotic ointment
- Burn medication
- Multi-vitamins
- Butterfly closures, Steri-strips, surgical or super glue, staples, and/or sutures
- Extra masks (both N95 and standard)
- Gloves for treating medical wounds. Nitrile is best. Get a full box, as they are handy for all sorts of things.
- Antiviral medicines such as Tamiflu
- Potassium iodide (KIO4) tablets
- Benadryl or allergy medicines
- Contraception if needed
- Anti-nausea medicine
- Electrolyte drinks or homemade electrolyte powders
- Braces for sprains
- Moleskins for foot relief
- Stethoscope (if you know how to use one)
- Gloves – both Nitrile and heavier gloves for those 'eaaau' moments
- Duct tape – lots of duct tape
- Potassium iodide capsules
- Snake bite kit
- Anti-diarrhea medication (for adults and children)
- Antibiotics
- Stool softeners
- Petroleum jelly or other lubricant
- CPR mask
- Colloidal silver
- Tweezers
- Tape
- Aspirin
- Sterile eye wash
- Cold/flu tablets

- Vitamins – especially vitamin C tablets
- Kleenex
- Feminine hygiene supplies
- Disposable hand wipes
- First aid instruction book

**If the above list is intimidating, here's another, shorter list that may suit you better**

- 2 ACE bandages
- 1 box of adhesive bandages of varying sized including at least two 2-inch or larger square bandages
- 6 butterfly bandages
- 1 large roll of 2-inch adhesive tape
- Several 4x4 inch sterile, non-adhesive dressings
- At least three rolls of 3-inch wide gauze
- At least two triangular bandages
- 2 tubes triple antibiotic ointment
- 1 box of alcohol wipes
- 1 box of two cold-packs
- Safety pins
- Scissors
- 1 box Nitrile gloves
- Variety of pain reliever tablets (aspirin, acetaminophen, etc.)
- Anti diarrhea medication
- Snakebite kit – especially if you live in an area where snakes are common
- Bottle of burn gel
- Bottle of calamine lotion (good for poison oak)

Here's the list I made for a particular group you may like as well:

First aid kits have a habit of ending up in all sorts of odd places but never where you need them during an emergency. We suggest you build three or four separate kits: a small one for Every Day Carry (EDC) such as in your purse, briefcase, or in your desk at work, one mid-sized kit in each vehicle, and one more complete kit at home. Having more than one first aid kit means one should be available where ever you may be when disaster strikes.

Kits are available commercially and you are encouraged to study them to find one that meets your needs. However, it is sometimes more practical to build your own that can be individualized to meet your family's needs.

The following lists will give you ideas for a basic kit. Note there is some redundancy in the lists, but that's necessary if they are to be stored in different locations.

### Make-It-Yourself First Aid Kits

**Purse pack** – part of your EDC (Every day carry)
      10 antiseptic wipes
      10-15 assorted band-aids
      Needle, scissors, fine-point tweezers
      1 pair Nitrile gloves
      1 roll of elastic bandage
      3 small gauze squares
      Steri-strips
      Several Q-tips
      Aspirin
      Ant- diarrhea medication
      Personal medications

**Basic First Aid Kit** - keep in your car
      Antiseptic wipes  (alcohol wipes)
      Antiseptic solution such as betadine
      Triple antibiotic ointment
      Burn medication (Burn Free)
      Band-aids (lots of different sizes)
      Roller bandages (gauze)
      Elastic bandages (roll)
      Sterile gauze (4 inch squares are best)
      Triangular bandages
      Butterfly closures, Steri-strips, surgical or super glue

Several N95 masks
Box of Nitrile gloves
Duct tape
Snake bit kit
Anti-diarrhea medication (for both adults and children)
2 boxes of instant cold packs (two packs to a box)
Oil of cloves (for toothaches)
Needle, scissors, fine-point tweezers
Q-tips
Acetaminophen tablets or ibuprofen
Antiseptic hand cleaner
Insect bite swabs
Triangular bandage
Barrier device for CPR
Medical adhesive tape
Flashlight with extra batteries

### Family of Four Home First Aid Kit

Multiple antiseptic wipes  (alcohol wipes)
1 bottle antiseptic solution such as betadine
2 tubes triple antibiotic ointment
2 tubes burn medication such as Burn Free
Band-aids (lots of different sizes)
2 boxes gauze roller bandages
2 boxes elastic bandages (roll) one 3 inches wide, one 4 inches wide
4 sterile gauze packets - both 3 inch and 4 inch squares)
2 Triangular bandages
1 packet of absorbent compress dressings (5x9 inches)
2 triangular bandages
Butterfly closures, Steri-strips, surgical or super glue
Several N95 masks – depending upon the size of your family
1 box of Nitrile gloves
D1 roll duct tape
Snake bit kit
Anti-diarrhea medication (for both adults and children)
2 boxes of instant cold packs (two packs to a box)

Oil of cloves (for toothaches)
Needle, scissors, fine-point tweezers
Q-tips
Acetaminophen tablets or ibuprofen
Aspirin .81 mg tablets
Hydrocortisone ointment
Antiseptic hand cleaner
Insect bite swabs
Barrier device for CPR (with one-way valve)
Medical adhesive tape
Flashlight with extra batteries
One oral thermometer (non-mercury, non-glass)
1-2 emergency blankets
1 bottle of calamine lotion
1 bottle of Pepto-Bismol
First aid instruction booklet

## Forms:

These forms can be downloaded as letter-size .pdf files from my website www.emergencyprepday.com

*In Case of Emergency*

*How You Can Find Me*

*Home Inventory*

*Pet Identification*

# In Case of Emergency

Name: _____   Date: _____

Address: _____

Phone: _____

## If you can't reach me at home, please try the following:

| | Name | Phone | Email |
|---|---|---|---|
| 1 | _____ | _____ | _____ |
| 2 | _____ | _____ | _____ |
| 3 | _____ | _____ | _____ |

Our Family Rendezvous Point is: _____

## Medial Information

| | Doctor | Phone | Location |
|---|---|---|---|
| 1 | _____ | _____ | _____ |
| 2 | _____ | _____ | _____ |

| | Insurance | | Policy Number |
|---|---|---|---|
| 1 | _____ | _____ | _____ |
| 2 | _____ | _____ | _____ |

## Other Information

| Attorney | Phone | Email |
|---|---|---|
| _____ | _____ | _____ |

| Person with Power of Attorney | Phone | Email |
|---|---|---|
| _____ | _____ | _____ |

Clergy

_____   _____   _____

## NOTES

## How You Can Find Me

**Home Information**

Names: _____

Street Address: _____

City: _____ State: _____ Zipcode: _____

Home Phone: _____ Cell Phone _____ Cell Phone #2 _____

Email _____ OR _____

Neighbors Name/Address/Phone _____

Neighbors Name/Address/Phone

**Employment Information**

Employer: _____

Address: _____

City: _____ State: _____ Zipcode: _____

Phone: _____ Phone _____

Email: _____ Website _____

**Employment Information**

Employer: _____

Address: _____

City: _____ State: _____ Zipcode: _____

Phone: _____ Phone _____

Email: _____ Website _____

**Other Contacts**

Other People Who Might Know Where I Am:

Name: _____ Phone: _____

Name: _____ Phone: _____

Name: _____ Phone: _____

Name: _____ Phone: _____

Name: _____ Phone: _____

**NOTES**

## Home Inventory

| Name: | Date: |
|---|---|
| Address: | Page: _____ of _____ |
| Phone: | Room: |

| Item | Serial Number | Description | Purchase Date | Value |
|---|---|---|---|---|
| | | | | |
| | | | | |
| | | | | |
| | | | | |
| | | | | |
| | | | | |
| | | | | |
| | | | | |
| | | | | |
| | | | | |
| | | | | |
| | | | | |
| | | | | |
| | | | | |
| | | | | |
| | | | | |
| | | | | |
| | | | | |
| | | | | |
| | | | | |
| | | | | |
| | | | | |
| | | | | |
| | | | | |

| NOTES |
|---|
| |

# Pet Emergency Information

Name: _____   Date: _____

Address: _____   Page: _____ of _____

Phone: _____   Total Number of Pets _____

## Veterinary Information

**Regular Veterinarian:**

Name: _____   Clinic Name: _____

Address: _____

Phone: _____   Emergency Phone _____

**Emergency Veterinarian / 24 Hour Hospital**

Name: _____   Clinic Name: _____

Address: _____

Phone: _____   Emergency Phone _____

## Pet Information

**Pet's Name:** _____   ☐ Male   ☐ Female

**Species** (Dog/Cat/etc) _____   **Breed** (Type) _____

**Color & Distiguishing Marks** _____   _____

**Collar and Tag ID?**   ☐ Ys ☐   Info: _____

**Implanted ID Chip?**   ☐ Ys ☐   Info: _____

**Does this animal bite?**   ☐ Ys ☐   Info: _____

**Allergies?**   ☐ Ys ☐   Info: _____

**Medical Problems?**   ☐ Ys ☐   Info: _____

**Attachments:**   ☐ Proof of Vaccinations

☐ Photocopies of Tags

☐ Insurance Information

☐ Additional Photos

☐ Copy of Medical Records

☐ Copy of Pedigree Papers

### NOTES

Attach Photo Here

© 2014, Emergency Prep Lady

# 500 Words or Less:  Articles from the Column, "Just in Case"

### #1 Office Rumblings! Now What?

You are working at your desk when you hear a distant rumbling. It's not a train, a plane, nor your office mate's stomach announcing lunch time. The building starts to shake, the lights go out, and you realize your worst fears: it's an earthquake. Not in Chile or Timbuktu, but right here in Gig Harbor! You dive under your desk as debris is falling from the ceiling, bookcases tip over, glass is breaking and dust fills the air. Chaos reigns supreme. Now what?

Stay calm and, at least for the moment, stay put!  Many people give in to their 'fight or flight' instinct and run. However, studies prove that many people are killed or injured as they run out of homes or offices when windows are breaking, masonry is falling and power lines are crashing to the sidewalks. Wait until the quaking stops then exit if you can do so safely.

If you are trapped inside a building or under your desk, a 72-hour kit could save your life or at least allow you to wait in relative comfort for rescue. However, if you haven't taken the time to put together your kit, you could be stuck without food or water for hours, if not for several days!

What kinds of items should be in your office e-kit? I suggest you personalize your kit rather than using standard lists available on the Internet. I have some items in mine that you might think unnecessary: heart meds, fingernail clippers, and lemon drops. However, a small blanket, a whistle, first aid kit, a flashlight with extra batteries, high-energy bars, dust masks, and a portable radio are necessities. Select a flashlight that uses the same size batteries as your radio. That way, spare batteries are always the right size.

If trapped, blow your whistle in three sharp blasts to let people know where you are. Three of anything is considered an emergency signal.

Don't yell for help because you don't want to fill your lungs with dust-filled air.

An office emergency kit should be sufficiently large to hold necessary items, but small enough to fit in a corner or under a desk without being obtrusive. A separate, more complete 72-hour pack should be created for your car in the event you are able to exit the building after the shaking stops.

Plan, purchase and practice: these are the keys to preparing for a disaster. However, remember that disaster preparedness is more than simply stockpiling water, food, and gear. It is also the determination to put those supplies where they will be needed and to develop the mental preparation to allow you to maintain control in out-of-control situations.

### #2 Protect Family Mementos: Buy a Scanner

Wildfires. They're unpredictable, frightening, and often extremely costly. This summer, firefighters are courageously battling fires throughout the Western states. Thousands of acres and hundreds of structures have been burned.

One massive out-of-control blaze was the Taylor Bridge fire near Cle Elum, just east of Seattle. Hundreds were ordered to evacuate. Some sat in shelters, unsure if the fires had spared their homes. At least forty-eight learned their homes had been consumed.

Some of the worst things a family can lose are those items that insurance can't replace: family mementos such as photo albums, a daughter's footprint taken when she was three days old, and the picture of great-grandfather in his Civil War uniform.

One evacuee commented on the evening news: "My home is gone. I have insurance that will cover most things, but I can't replace my daughter's baby pictures." I felt sorry for him, but I was also frustrated because it was an unnecessary loss.

Why was it an unnecessary loss? Because it would have taken only a few dollars and perhaps one afternoon to insure that all his precious photos were protected.

We live in a fragile world where disasters, widespread or personal, happen with startling regularity. Wildfires create havoc every summer. An electrical fire or forgotten candle can cause a home to burn to the ground, destroying all contents.

The prudent person invests in insurance to cover these occurrences, but what about items which are irreplaceable? The answer is simple: plan ahead. Invest in a scanner.

Scanners range in price from about $100 for a simple flatbed scanner to 'ohmigosh' for one that does everything except wash the dog or take out the garbage.

Buy a scanner and scan all your treasured photos. Scan the not-so-treasured photos as well, such as those old albums that you've stored in the attic, the antique postcards from Aunt Nellie, or the stacks of photos that languish in your desk drawer.

Also scan important documents: marriage and birth certificates, college diplomas, military discharge papers, deeds and wills, passports, and other documents that prove your identity.

Once the scanning has been accomplished, download the images to a password protected disk and make several copies. Give copies to trusted relatives, preferably who live out of state. Store a copy with your 72-hour pack or bug-out bag. If disaster strikes, you can recreate your photos and important documents from the disks.

Yes, it's time consuming to remove photos from frames, scan them, and then return them to their place of honor. It takes dedication and determination to scan albums and stacks of miscellaneous photos.

However, which would you prefer: a few hours of repeatedly hitting a scan button or years of regret for cherished mementos that were irrevocably lost?

We tend to think that nothing of this sort will ever happen to us, but it can…and it does.

The fellow from Cle Elum has only scattered memories of his daughter's childhood. Learn from his regrets. Scan those irreplaceable family mementos now…just in case!

### #3  Chicken or Hen?

My friends call me a chicken! Not the Marty McFly type, as I'm really brave about having adventures or traveling alone. With emergency preparedness, however, I'm either Chicken Little or the Little Red Hen. You must decide which!

Hopefully, you know the stories, but let me refresh your memory. When an acorn fell on Chicken Little's head, she thought the sky was falling. That phrase, "The sky is falling" developed into a common idiom indicating a hysterical or mistaken belief that disaster is imminent.

The Little Red Hen was the original preparedness chick. She found some grains of wheat and decided to be prudent. "Who will help me…?" is the phrase repeated throughout the story. Her friends, the pig, the horse, etc. would not help as she planted, watered, weeded, harvested, and ground the grain until she said, "Who will help me eat the bread?" Then, of course, they all wanted to participate. "Nope," said Little Red Hen, "I'll do it myself," as she proceeded to feed herself and her little brood of baby chicks!

Now to the serious stuff.  We live near "the most dangerous volcano in the United States". Gig Harbor sits serenely near several earthquake faults. We live near military bases, major seaports, and an international border. We've experienced 9/11, watched TV coverage of disasters from New Orleans to Haiti. Yet, few have complied with the recommendations made by numerous organizations promoting basic, prudent steps to ensure our safety in the event of a mega-disaster.

We rush to assist strangers who are victims of far-flung disasters but we are generally not sufficiently motivated to prepare ourselves and our families for a major emergency that could occur right here in Gig Harbor! We stubbornly believe that disasters only happen to other people in other places....not to us! Someone recently told me that in a major emergency, she would just call 911. It never occurred to her that 350,000 other people might be doing the same thing!

General disaster readiness calls for a minimum of a three day supply of food and water. However, most groups recommend supplies for three weeks to three months. I recently heard a FEMA executive state quite firmly that in the event of a major disaster, FEMA would take at least three days just to arrive in the state. Then he added, "And we won't be coming to Gig Harbor. We'll go where we can do the most good for the most people:  Seattle, Tacoma, Olympia."

In an emergency, we in Gig Harbor must rely upon ourselves, our neighbors, and our local first responders. In a large-scale disaster, the average citizen may end up being a first responder for an extended period of time as the usual emergency systems become overwhelmed or incapacitated. That's why individual and family preparedness planning is so crucial in disaster readiness.

So, one can be a Chicken Little, Little Red Hen or perhaps an ostrich looking for sand. I know which I am. Which are you?

**#4**  A Great Feeling...Food on the Table.

Recently I asked this question: How would you feel if you rushed to the grocery store for desperately needed supplies only to find the shelves virtually empty? Did you wonder if that could happen right here in River City?  Okay, I'll put the musical reference aside. Could it happen right here in Gig Harbor? Did you consider putting some supplies aside 'just in case'? Or did you snort, "Nah, that couldn't happen in Gig Harbor."

Oh, but it could! Easily! Have you ever been to a grocery store at the onset of a severe storm? I have...and it's spooky! There were panicked people everywhere trying to get food. Imagine what would happen if there was news of an earthquake, flood, or ice storm that would disrupt the flow of supplies for a prolonged period of time. Empty shelves!

Basic necessities disappear quickly during a crisis and it doesn't take much to trigger a buying frenzy that could strip the shelves bare. Even if limited supplies are available, do you really want to risk the health of your family by 'hoping' that all will be well?

When a crisis arises, <u>you</u> must provide for your family. You cannot rely on the government, your church, or the Red Cross to do so. FEMA folks urge families to prepare basic supplies to sustain them for at least three weeks. Fortunately, it isn't terribly difficult to stockpile sufficient groceries for a few weeks. So where do you start?

First, utilizing canned or packaged goods, select two menus each for breakfast, lunch and dinner.  For example, choose hot oatmeal cereal with dried fruit and hot chocolate for one breakfast, pancakes with Spam for the second. Next, purchase sufficient supplies to serve these six meals to your family <u>seven</u> times. Voila! You have a two-week supply of basic meals. Next, add two choices of snacks to round of the basic menu. When that is accomplished, pat yourself on the back. You've done well…but you aren't finished yet.

Choose another set of six meals and repeat the process. This will provide your family with four weeks of guaranteed food. Four weeks! Sounds good, doesn't it?  But, you ask, what about perishable items like milk, eggs, butter, and cheese?  These are available in freeze dried or dehydrated packages that you can simply store with your other nonperishable goods. They may not taste as nice as fresh, but it's better than doing without. Utilize your freezer as well. Butter and bacon, for example, freeze quite well for short periods of time.

Don't just 'buy and forget'. Your supplies must be rotated to remain viable. If you have selected menus that your family eats regularly, rotation won't be a problem. Just use the old and replace it with new.

Just imagine the peace of mind you'll enjoy by knowing that no matter what happens, your family will have sufficient food to eat for at least four weeks.  Now that's a great feeling!

### #5 Where Are Your Kids?

Have you ever lost a child? I did once. On a dark, cold, December evening, through a series of miscommunications, I feared my eight-year-old daughter had been left alone at Tacoma Mall. For a terrifying thirty minutes, I didn't know where she was or if she was safe. Those few minutes scarred my psyche forever. Fortunately, I found her at a friend's home, but I'll never forget the experience.

Can you imagine the sheer terror of not knowing where your children are or if they are safe? The very thought makes my heart flutter and my mouth go dry. It's unthinkable, yet in a disaster, that's exactly what can happen.

If a major earthquake struck Gig Harbor, normal communications could be virtually nonexistent. Land-line phone service could be lost, and cellular service would be so overloaded, it could take two hours to get a line and then you could only use the line for a brief moment....if you can get through at all.

If the event occurs during school hours, educators are instructed to allow children to leave the school only with a pre-registered family member. If bridges and overpasses have collapsed and roads are impassable, how will you reach your children? How long would it take to walk to the school? How would you communicate your plans to your children?

These questions beg for answers. Therefore, I suggest you play the "what if..?" game with your children to prepare them for a situation where communication between parent and child is limited or nonexistent.

First, designate an out-of-state contact as it may be easier to make a long-distance phone call than to call across town. The contact person can relay messages between local family members. Each family member should memorize the contact's phone number, but since memory sometimes fails in an emergency, also create a contact card for each to keep in a wallet, purse, or backpack. Send one with each child to their school to keep on file there as well. Teach your children...or have them teach you...to send text messages. Texting will often go through when calls won't. If your children have a cell phone, program the contact number as "ICE" (In Case of Emergency).

Second, plan for the emergency. Will Mom or Dad be closest to the school? Who will walk, if driving is impossible, to get the kiddies? If your youngest goes to Voyager and your eldest attends Kopachuck, do you want them to be together until you arrive? If so, make written arrangements with the school in advance. The school must have the names of anyone who is authorized to pick up your children.

Just like fire drills, planning...then practicing... for an emergency will not eliminate the disaster, but it will make the event more manageable and less frightening. Make e-prep a family affair; let the children help plan, prepare, and practice! Where children's safety is concerned, you must leave nothing to chance.

### #6 Ability to Build a Fire is Key to Survival

There are five basic needs one must consider to survive an emergency situation: warmth, shelter, water and food, communication, and first aid.

Let's consider the first: warmth. The ability to build a fire is crucial. A well built fire will provide light and warmth, cook food, purify water, dry clothes, comfort the soul, and keep away things that go bump in the night.

Unfortunately, making a fire isn't a matter of simply striking a match and holding it to a piece of wood. Often, available tinder is damp or green. Windy, cold, wet conditions can further complicate attempts to start a fire, as can exhaustion, injury or inexperience.
Experts recommend survival kits contain multiple ways to kindle a blaze. I suggest matches, lighters, and fire-steel.

Matches are inexpensive, but have a shelf life of only several years so must be rotated. Old matches may not light, especially if they have been exposed to dampness. Even waterproof matches may not light under very wet conditions.

Tip: bundle several matches together, tie with cotton thread, and then dip in melted paraffin or recycled candle wax. Carry several of these bundles in zip-lock bags. They are more efficient than a single match.

Butane lighters are handy and light weight, but their fuel has limited shelf life. They may leak and working parts may fail, so are only a short term solution for starting fires. Pack several but check them often.

Flint and steel, or fire-steel, is almost a perfect fire starter. It can get soaking wet and still produce sparks. One fire-steel can light thousands of fires and has unlimited shelf life. They are available at the most sporting goods stores or online.

Fire-steels work best when you catch the produced sparks in some kind of dry, fuzzy material. Cotton ball fire starters work beautifully and can be easily made at home.
Roll cotton balls in petroleum jelly until completely covered, then store in a zip-lock bag. When needed, loosely pull apart about three balls so air can flow freely, place them under dry kindling, then shower sparks from your fire-steel onto the cotton.

A homemade fire stick can help kindle a blaze even in soggy conditions. To make a fire stick, cut corrugated cardboard into six inch strips about two inches wide. Roll tightly and secure with cotton yarn, then submerge in melted wax. Make sure the wax permeates the cardboard. Let cool, then dip again. Two or three of these sticks will start a fire even with green wood.

Just because you carry fire starting materials does not mean your attempts will be successful. Gather the necessary materials and then practice until you become expert with each method.

Building a fire is an extremely important survival skill and should be learned in advance…not during a disaster when stress levels are high.

Remember, your ability to create fire may be a lifesaver during unexpected situations.

Plan, purchase, and practice. A disaster may be lurking just around the corner.

### #7 Dare to Prepare for an Emergency

"I dare you." Growing up, I hated that phrase, especially when it came from my sister. I always took the dare and it always got me into trouble. If I resisted her taunts, she borrowed a line from "A Christmas Story" and would 'double-dog dare' me. That was impossible to resist.

I hope you can't resist it either. Therefore, I double-dog dare you to try an experiment. The rules are simple: pretend your area has experienced a disaster which requires you to survive without any public services for 24 hours.

That means water doesn't magically flow at the turn of a tap, flicking a light switch doesn't illuminate the room, there is no TV, no computer, no microwave, and no stove. All cell phones, kindles, iPods, etc. are off-limits.

Without water, how will you flush your toilets? Wash dishes? Boil macaroni or mix concentrated orange juice?

Without power, how will you cook a hot meal? Light and heat your home? Know what is happening in your immediate area or in the world? Entertain your children?

What items might you gather before you spring this experiment on your unsuspecting family? Candles are nice; lanterns even better. Batteries are a necessity for both flashlights and portable radios. Paper plates? Chocolate?

A deck of cards or board games might come in handy, as well as coloring books and crayons for younger children. How about Mountain

House meals that only require boiling water or other foods that require little cooking?

Cooking without power can be a challenge. Do you have camping gear that could be utilized? Sterno stoves? Have you made buddy burners from tuna cans, cardboard, and candle wax?

Did you know that hand sanitizer contains similar ingredients to sterno? It's actually a great fire starter or accelerant. It doesn't burn as long as the thicker sterno, but if your sterno can is low, add some hand sanitizer to continue cooking.

What drinking water do you have readily available? If you have extra room in your freezer, use the space to store water in plastic jugs. It will help keep your freezer cold during a power outage and when it melts, can be used for drinking or cooking.

Rain water can be used to flush toilets or for washing. However, you must have a way to collect this valuable…and free…resource. To create a catchment system, place a barrel under a down spout. Install a mesh filter on the barrel to prevent unwanted materials from entering the barrel. I added a bit of whimsy to my system by attaching a dragon gargoyle to the downspout. He now spurts into my rain barrel.

In a real disaster, there is no choice as to whether or not to participate, nor is there time to correct any deficiencies. You can, however, choose to create your own 'trial run'. Such an experiment will help determine what preparations are necessary to ensure the safety and welfare of your family during an emergency.

So….I double-dog dare you to do it.


## #8 Living Prepared for Emergencies

If I can share one small bit of advice, it is this: everyone should be prepared for the unexpected. We never know when some emergency or disaster will occur. Preparedness, therefore, is vitally important. Why am I so adamant about this? Because I've been there, done that, and I don't want to do it again.

I've experienced an earthquake in Costa Rica when all my emergency supplies were at home; I was woefully unprepared.

I've been stuck on the I-5 freeway between Seattle and Tacoma in a raging snowstorm in someone else's car. My 'stuff' was in my car; I was again unprepared.

After those uncomfortable experiences, I vowed to never be in that situation again. I learned to 'live prepared' at all times. Living prepared means <u>always</u> having basic emergency supplies within reach.

Does this mean you have to tote around a huge backpack everywhere you go? No, of course not, but you can have a few basics in your purse, pack, and in your car and office.

Start with the simple things. Attach whistles and small flashlights to all key chains, backpacks, or zippers on frequently worn jackets, and to the headboard of each bed.
Tuck basic necessities into your purse or pack. A space blanket takes up less space than a pack of cigarettes, and is far more beneficial. Add a small knife to your key ring. Stash a water bottle, a couple of high energy bars, and a dust mask in your desk at work.

Assemble a bed bag for each family member. Include items needed in the first 15 minutes after an earthquake such as shoes and socks, warm clothing, hat, gloves, water, high energy bars, dust mask, goggles, and necessary medications.

Food storage is as important as a savings account. Build it in the same way…little by little. Learn to store what you eat and eat what you store. Rotation is the key to a successful program.

Inventory your pantry, and then buy a few extra items each time you shop for groceries. Over time, it will add up and soon you'll have a three-week supply of meals for the family.

Use empty soda-pop bottles to store water or keep bottled water on hand. Don't use fruit or milk jugs as they can harbor bacteria no matter how well they are washed.

Can you afford it? Yes. It is a misconception that it takes a ton of cash to prepare for emergencies. It takes planning, effort, and commitment, but much can be accomplished with only a modest outlay of cash. Purchasing a little bit here and there doesn't affect the family budget drastically.

Make emergency preparedness a family priority. Create a plan, set goals, and get started. It will surprise you how quickly you can gather necessary supplies.

Being prepared for emergencies equates with self-reliance, confidence, comfort, and peace of mind.  It does take effort and determination however, in an emergency or a disaster, you'll be grateful you learned to 'live prepared.'

### #9 Lessons from the Past Assist with Future Emergencies

I'm convinced that as we mature, the follies of our youth come back to haunt us.  At eighteen, smashing my knee sky-diving was no big deal. Now, however, arthritis troubles me constantly.  Have I learned from past mistakes?  Of course not.  Recently, I tore my rotator cuff trying to emulating Ziva's knife-throwing skill. Geeez!

However, I have occasionally learned from the experiences of others, such as Elspeth.  In the late 50's, Elspeth was a successful runway model and the darling of all the designers in Paris. She was beautiful, smart, and quite willing to help convince designers to hire me for Paris Collections.

She taught me a great deal, but the most memorable lesson wasn't about modeling.  It was her experiences in German-occupied France that impressed me. Her stories of severe deprivations during World War II shaped my attitudes towards emergency preparedness.

I learned, vicariously, the harsh realities of food shortages, lack of basic necessities, and how seemingly simple items can become desperately important and almost unattainable.

In war-torn Europe, fine soap was rare. Some lucky households had fats and caustic soda, so made soap that was highly valued, even though it was rough and corrosive to the skin.
Cooking oil was the single most sought after item. Fat is a necessary part of one's diet as it allows the absorption of nutrients that require fat in order to metabolize in the body. Not only does it infuse fats into the diet, but without it, food either burns or must be boiled. From Elspeth, I learned to include these items in my emergency storage.

Oils are sensitive to heat, light, and oxygen so must be kept in a cool, dark place. Refined oils high in monounsaturated fats will keep about a year. Unrefined polyunsaturated oils don't store well, while olive oil will keep several years unopened and about nine months after opening. Don't discard out-dated or rancid oil. It can be used in oil lamps.

Stockpile your soap in a dark area that isn't exposed to extreme shifts in humidity and temperature. Place soaps in cardboard boxes lined with recycled brown paper bags. Cut ventilation holes in the sides so the soap is protected from light and dust but still gets some air.

Don't store soap in sealed plastic storage boxes or bags. Soap containing lye will turn rancid if enclosed in plastic. Soap that is exposed to high humidity gets slimy as the glycerin in soap attracts moisture from the air.

Include in your storage plans things that provide comfort; those products that make us feel more human. Items such as toothpaste, shampoo or chocolate may help reduce stress in traumatic situations.

Don't wait until after an event to learn by sad experience what you should have stored. Learn from the experiences of others; it's far less painful.

I think Elspeth would be pleased to know that lavender-scented soap, face cream, hand lotion and lemon drops are included in my storage plan. And, of course, lots of olive oil.

## #10  CERT – Much More Than a Breath Mint

Ah, Certs. The breath mint with its signature green flecks has been popular since its debut in 1956. You might remember their ad campaign: "Two…two…two mints in one!" A breath mint and a candy mint. Delightful.

To those in emergency planning, however, CERT has different meaning. It's an acronym for Community Emergency Response Team: a program that trains volunteers in emergency response skills such as fire safety, light search and rescue, triage and first aid.

Following a major disaster, FEMA predicts that emergency services will not be able to meet the immediate needs of the community. There would be too many victims and too few responders. Additionally, roads may be blocked; bridges and overpasses may have collapsed, isolating Gig Harbor from the rest of the state.

When every minute counts and lives are at stake, people may need to rely on each other for immediate help. But are you or your neighbors trained to handle life-threatening situations?

For example, do you know how to use leverage and cribbing to lift a fallen wall that has trapped a child? How do you treat these three killers: blocked airways, uncontrolled bleeding, and shock? Do you have the necessary supplies? Do you know basic triage methods?

CERT teaches these and many other life-saving skills. It enables volunteers to quickly and efficiently do a great deal of good for a great number of people. To my mind, CERT members are heroes.

Years ago, I didn't have a clue what to do in situations where emergency help was needed. Nevertheless, I volunteered during several natural disasters simply because I wanted to help. This may be an admirable response, yet it can also be deadly. In the Mexico City earthquake, untrained, spontaneous volunteers rescued over 800 people, but nearly 100 of them lost their lives while attempting to save others.

Specialized training in emergency management can prevent many such deaths. CERT teaches its leaders how to organize both members and spontaneous volunteers in order to provide necessary aid without placing themselves in danger.

CERT members are taught what to expect following a major disaster, how to assess immediate needs, and how to collect disaster intelligence to assist professional responders in saving lives. The volunteers develop the essential skills to manage a multitude of situations that would be daunting to the untrained.

CERT is about people helping people. The program, authorized under FEMA and Citizens Corp, instructs everyday citizens how to make a difference, how to help themselves, their families, their neighbors and their communities in troubled times.

Take the training; join the team. It's challenging, rewarding, and fun. You'll learn new skills and meet interesting people. Best of all, you'll be prepared to assist our community when disaster strikes.

Community Emergency Responses Teams are valuable assets to our community. CERTS are heroes…not breath mints.

### #11 The Sharp Edge of Emergency Preparation… Knives!

I've fallen in love. Oh, not the romantic type…I'm far too old for that. Rather, I've fallen in love with Big Five, specifically the section where they display knives. I find something irresistible on every visit. That place is as addicting as peanut butter!

First, I bought a tiny pocket knife that's perfect for my key ring and a larger fold-up knife for my pack. Next, they had these amazing survival knives on sale that I just couldn't resist. I found a large Bowie knife, a HumVee set, and then… Well, you get the picture.

In times past, practically everyone carried a pocket knife. It was useful for peeling an orange, quartering an apple, or any other random task. Old men would whittle small toys for children: whistles, dolls, and games. Today, children want video games rather than hand made whistles. Also, with increased security concerns, we've generally stopped carrying knives.

It's unfortunate. A knife is handy for opening packages or envelopes, removing splinters, slicing lemons, cutting string, or making a sandwich. It is doubly practical in emergency situations.

Emergencies are, by their very nature, unforeseen. Since our goal is to be prepared for the unexpected, one should always have easy access to a knife. This important tool should be in your 72-hour pack, on your key ring, in your car and home…and where possible, in your pocket or purse.

In my not-so-humble opinion, no one should leave home without a survival knife. It's the perfect multifunction survival tool. The saw tooth portion of the blade can be used to cut wood for shelter or firewood. Inside the hollow handle are matches with a strike pad, wire ring saw, needles, and emergency fishing supplies, including fish hook, lead shot, and nylon line.

I also recommend carrying a pocket knife with multiple tools such as a screwdriver, bottle opener, blade and pliers. In an emergency, you may suddenly need one of these tools, such as after an auto accident when seatbelts won't release.

For an emergency pack, select at least two fixed-blade knives of different sizes, preferably with a full tang. The tang of a knife is the portion of the blade that extends down into the handle. A full tang…or tang that goes all the way to the base of the handle, gives the knife additional strength.

Before you decide to carry a knife, consider local laws. There are restrictions on blade length, types of blade, open assist mechanisms, and concealed carry requirements. Check with the your local police department for specifics before making a purchase. Word to the wise: most school districts strictly prohibit any knives on school property.

Most everyone knows what knives are for. Recently, however, I was asked this question: Why on earth would a little old lady like you carry a knife? Smiling, I gave the obvious answer: A knife is good to keep the zombies out of my peanut butter. After all, you just never know when a peanut butter zombie might show up.

### #12 Disaster, Like Beauty, is in the Eye of the Beholder

Exactly what constitutes a disaster for which we should be prepared? Is it an 8.4 earthquake, a devastating tsunami, or a horrific ice storm? Or can it be something of a more personal nature, like the loss of a job, a small fender-bender, or just one of the myriad of events that can, at least temporarily, spoil our day?

A small child once called 911 in a panic. "I missed the school bus," she sobbed to the responder. Later, her mother asked why she called 911. The child answered, "You told me to call it if there was an emergency." To her, this was a genuine calamity.

A disaster is defined by those experiencing the problem. Chances are that 90% of you will experience in the near future some adversity that could qualify as a disaster, however minor. Hopefully, it will be nothing more than a cut from a broken glass or an inconvenient flat tire. These aren't disasters in the true sense of the word, but for the person involved, it certainly isn't a picnic.

When I speak about emergency preparedness, I generally address major events and, to be honest, most of my personal preparation is geared towards these kinds of situations. So far, I have not had to utilize my supplies for a major catastrophe…thank goodness! I have, however, been called upon to offer my supplies for events others considered at least small disasters.

For example, a teacher at a Gig Harbor school had an unexpected collision with a food tray which resulted in her shirt being covered with spaghetti, salad, and ranch dressing.

"I'm so glad you were subbing here today," she told me as she gratefully accepted a clean shirt. "I knew you'd have something in your van I could wear."

Recently there was a minor accident involving a pedestrian and a car. The pedestrian, an elderly man, lay on the sidewalk, shaken but not seriously injured. He was comforted by a blanket and airline pillow from my van as we waited for the ambulance.

Being a preparedness person, my van is fairly well-stocked with these types of items, including several inexpensive umbrellas. It's amazing how many times I've offered umbrellas to people caught by an unexpected downpour, although how rain can be unexpected in the Pacific Northwest is beyond my comprehension.

I advocate preparedness, not only for major disasters that may lurk somewhere in our future, but for the smaller, every-day inconveniences that plague each and every one of us. If we prepare for the Big One, we are prepared for nearly anything that may happen: a broken fingernail, (nail clippers and emery boards), a sudden headache (Tylenol), a small cut (band-aids and mouthwash to be used as an antiseptic) or for the more serious stuff such as auto accidents, storms, or a sudden craving for lemon drops.

Whether or not your area experiences a major disaster, general preparedness is the key to comfortably surviving all aspects of our lives…including large or small disasters.

### #13 Ten Tips for Emergency Preparedness on a Budget

"I don't have the money to buy all that stuff."
"I know I should do the preparedness thing, but my budget is tight!"

Sound familiar? Money…or lack thereof…is often the primary explanation as to why many people don't prepare for emergencies. Okay, in reality, apathy is probably the top reason, but for our purposes today, let's pretend that money is the problem.

It takes cash to get prepared. Nevertheless, it is possible to work towards being well prepared even on a very tight budget. It requires planning, forethought, some sacrifice, and that terrible word: budgeting.

Still, the rewards are great. Preparedness changes confusion and chaos to confidence and control. There's even a scripture that reads, "If ye are prepared, ye shall not fear."

Trust me. If, or as the experts say, <u>when</u> a disaster occurs, you'll be grateful for whatever preparedness steps you've taken.

Here's a list of ten tips for starting emergency preparedness on a budget.

1.  Plan for the most likely disasters that can happen in the area where you live. Here in Gig Harbor, an earthquake is much more likely than a hurricane, trucking strikes more probable than a tornado. Plan accordingly.
2.  Create your own personalized list of supplies. Think where you may be when disaster strikes, what will you do, and what will you need with which to do it. Pre-made kits are available, but individualized, home-created kits are generally more complete.
3.  Make a checklist, then purchase carefully. Avoid impulse buys. Use your list to avoid duplicating non-food items.
4.  Make preparedness items a 'normal' expense of your budget. Normal expenses don't generally get cut, while 'extras' regularly get set aside.
5.  Buy one or more preparedness items each time you enter a grocery store. Even $20 per month can help add to your supplies.
6.  Save by shopping sales. Make use of coupons.
7.  Don't replace your emergency items annually. Replace and cycle through those items that have limited shelf life (e.g. batteries, food) regularly. Remember the rule: rotate, rotate, rotate.
8.  Store water in safe containers. It is not necessary to buy expensive bottled water, but make sure any containers used for water storage are safe and disinfected. Don't use milk jugs, but soda pop bottles are okay for short-term storage.

9.  Request 'prepper type' items as gifts.
10. Think ahead. You are more likely to save money if you can take your time with focused and strategic shopping. It's when everyone is at the store right before the storm hits that prices are higher and impulse buying rules the roost.

I know I said just ten tips, but here's one I must add. Trade a quick stop at the Golden Arches or a night out on the town for prepping supplies. One foray at a fast-food establishment can cost a family upwards of $50. That can fund lots of emergency supplies.

I realize budgets are tight, but to ignore emergency preparedness is to invite disaster.
Be prepared. It's worth the effort.

### #14  In A Disaster, Don't Come to My House!

Most of the time, I'm a fairly patient person. Most of the time, I'm a reasonably nice person...at least I hope so. Most of the time, I'm calm, controlled, and most definitely non-confrontational. Unfortunately, today isn't 'most of the time'.

Today, I'm very annoyed. There's actually a more succinct word that could be used instead of annoyed, but it is inappropriate for use by a white-haired little old lady.

Please let me explain.

Over the years I've been writing/speaking/teaching about emergency preparation, I've heard all sorts of lame excuses as to why some people do not bother to prepare for anything: not for a major or minor disaster, not for economic woes, not for any unexpected event.

"They won't let the economy fail...Earthquakes only happen in poor countries...Well, if something happens, the government will take care of us....Someone will provide for me...It's too much bother... If something happens, I'll just wing it!"

Unfortunately, these comments are invariably followed by the one statement that really infuriates me: "If something does happen, I'll just come to your house!"

Sorry, Charlie. It doesn't work that way.

If an earthquake strikes Gig Harbor, if our economy collapses and all heck breaks loose, if grocery stores shelves are suddenly stripped of all essentials, even if aliens land in Skansie Park, <u>don't come to my house</u>!

I'm still attempting to gather emergency supplies to meet the needs of my own family. I simply don't have the resources to store supplies for those who were warned but <u>chose</u> not to listen.

And, why should I? When does another's neglect become my responsibility? Too many people refuse to take responsibility for themselves and their families, expecting others to step up to the plate for them. Harsh as this may sound, the reality is this: where limited supplies are concerned, family will take precedence over friends and neighbors.

Churches and communities will attempt to help and yes, even the government, but the responsibility for meeting the basic needs of your family lies with you. Not with your church or neighbors and most assuredly not with me. You are responsible for your family's welfare.

For nearly two years, this column has given advice on all sorts of preparedness topics. I've listed reasons to prepare as well as ideas for storing food and water, ways to cook without power, and the importance of preparing for other basic needs: light, shelter, warmth, communications, and health/medical.

My goal is to help families prepare for emergencies. I write, speak, and teach about 'prepping' to anyone who will listen. I encourage everyone to develop plans and gather supplies. That's my job.

However, I can't make you prepare, nor can I prepare for you. That's <u>your</u> job.

Don't assume that in a disaster, others will have sufficient supplies to meet your needs. Instead, plan, purchase and prepare now for emergencies that may affect your family.

Remember, if you neglect to prepare and disaster strikes, you're on your own. Coming to my house is not an option.